MW01110213

Chemo Heart: Cancer, Resiliency and Seeing What's Essential

Mike Verano, LPC, LMFT, CEAP, DCC, CCISM

To Bob & Margaret

Hope Blooms!

Mike Ver

Cover by Ralph Verano
http://rverano.blogspot.com

"Here is my secret. It is very simple: It is only with the heart that one can see rightly; what is essential is invisible to the eye"

- Antoine de Saint Exupery, The Little Prince

This book is dedicated to my wife Kathy, the heart of my recovery, wellness and life beyond cancer.

The Heart of the Matter

Your vision will become clear only when you can look into your own heart. Who looks outside, dreams; who looks inside, awakes. – Carl Jung

"I was a better person while going through cancer treatment." While I knew, as a result of my counseling sessions with other cancer survivors, and from my own cancer treatment, what she meant, I asked the 26 year old breast cancer survivor to explain. "I was more focused on what's important," she added, "I wasn't stressing out over little things and I felt more appreciative."

Now, seven years into survivorship, I have a greater understanding of this paradox; this awful fate that had entered my life, brought with it an awareness of, and contact with, what is essential in life. It's clear to me now that woven into the very fabric of this dreaded disease are the tenuous fibers of compassion, empathy and love.

This is not to say that I'm a card-carrying member of the "cancer is the best thing that ever happened to me" club. I'm not and, as a matter of fact, I once toyed with the idea of creating a counter movement called, "If cancer is the best thing that ever happened to you, you need to look up the definition of best thing." Once I realized that the slogan was too unwieldy for coffee mugs, t-shirts or Internet memes, I shortened it to, "Cancer; been there, done that."

As a licensed therapist who spends much of his time rooting around the psyches of complete strangers and some of his free time in the dark recesses of my own, I've understand that it is not cancer that brings with it the gift of seeing through life meaningless minutia into the vast depths of the truly important. What cancer does provide is a doorway, a portal through which one can not only glimpse, but if one chooses, live a heart-centered existence.

Living with what I call chemo heart, is not the transformation into being a better person, per se, it is the awakening to the basic elements of a meaningful life, even if that life is in the throes of a threatening disease. This awakening is neither guaranteed nor inevitable. As anyone who has taken the cancer journey knows, the door that cancer opens swings both ways; on the one side isolation, desperation and despair await, on the other, communion, inspiration, and hope.

While I've heard from many cancer survivors that they gained a deeper sense of what is important, and felt transformed, I've also heard, and experienced first-hand, what I call the persistence of personality. This rebound to our pre-cancer selves is characterized by the return of petty concerns, acting out of mindless habit and feeling, once again alone and afraid in a terrifying world.

The great news is that chemo heart, like its evil twin chemo brain, is a byproduct of cancer treatment. Unlike chemo brain, the unwelcome guest that eats all your food, plays its music too loud and never picks up after itself, chemo heart is the demure houseguest who will not stay if not invited and leaves all to soon if the welcome mat is rolled up and put away.

When confronted by the question of what to do with the time spent while in the throes of cancer treatment and its recovery, I'm often reminded of the lines from the Pablo Neruda poem, *Time that was not lost*:

So many wings flew around
The mountains of sorrow
And so many wheels beat
The highway of our destiny,
We had nothing left to lose.
And our weeping ended.

Too often, when illness strikes we feel as if life is put on hold. We even talk about having lost time while sick or recovering. The notion is that our lives move in certain trajectories, and that ill health is a deviation from that course, has strong ties to our collection aversion to suffering.

This sense of time wasted, of a life that has jumped the track and is now stuck on the sidelines, adds an extra burden to our psyches. As cancer patients, we watch as healthy and vibrant people move with a care-free, seemingly orchestrated, ease. If we really want to push our grief deeper, we envy them and their nonchalant approach to their days. Secretly, in the deepest recesses of our hearts, lingers the unanswerable "Why me, why now, why this?"

But what if these moments do not represent a pause in life? What if they are not detours but a direct path? Less traveled, surely, but no less valuable than the well mapped out roads more desired? Is it possible that we were meant to live our illnesses with the same curiosity and willingness normally reserved for "the good life?"

There is no such thing as lost time. Illness does not take us out of the game; it pushes us deeply into the heart of the matter. Whether or not we experience gain or loss depends on whether our pain brings openings or shuts us off from being able to live life fully. Personally, I found that the door of awareness rests on loose hinges. At times, it swings easily into the realm of depression and "what ifs."

However, with the same ease, it opens on the vast experience of life in the now.

Sharing my experience helps me make sense of what I have been through, not by reliving it, but by living through it with others. If this experience has taught me anything it is that none of us goes it alone. I whole-heartedly believe that the path of my recovery is paved by the thoughts, prayers and healing energy of others. My hope is that by sharing this episode in my life I might repay some of the overwhelming kindness shown to me.

What follows is a guide to that path of recovery, an instruction manual from moving out of the mind-centered realm of side-effects and disease into to the primary experience of thriving with an open and loving heart.

A Chemo No-Brainer

Cancer can take away all of my physical abilities. It cannot touch my mind, it cannot touch my heart, and it cannot touch my soul. – Jim Valvano

Ask ten medical professionals whether or not chemo brain is real and you'll likely get a variety of answers. Ask ten cancer patients and the response might be, "Wait, what was the question? Oh yeah, chemo brain. You bet it's real!"

Whether it's the result of physiological changes, chemical imbalances or a stress response, chemo brain remains one of the inheritances of facing the cancer challenge.

The American Cancer Society describes the following as reported symptoms of chemo brain:

1. Forgetting things that they usually have no trouble recalling (memory lapses)

2. Trouble concentrating (they can't focus on what they're doing, have a short attention span, may "space out")

3. Trouble remembering details like names, dates, and sometimes larger events

4. Trouble multi-tasking, like answering the phone while cooking, without losing track of one task (they are less able to do more than one thing at a time)

5. Taking longer to finish things (disorganized, slower thinking and processing)

6. Trouble remembering common words (unable to find the right words to finish a sentence)

Sadly, we cancer survivors are often measured by what we've lost to cancer. Whether it's cognitive functioning, organs, body parts or even the illusion that we're invincible, cancer and its treatment, is fraught with minuses. Therefore, chemo heart is an attempt to put something back in the space left by all the things taken away.

Chemo heart (CH) manifests itself on the day we're diagnosed and progressively spreads the longer we face the challenge. CH is a condition of increasing awareness of one's true nature and the felt connection with the whole of life, characterized by:

1. Remembering to appreciate friends and loved ones

2. No trouble looking past small slights, slanders and insults

3. No trouble seeing past life's distracting minutia

4. No trouble making one's primary task to enjoy life

5. Taking one's time to linger over life's simple pleasures

6. No trouble remembering to honor others who are also facing this challenge

Unlike chemo brain, chemo heart puts us squarely in the plus column and acts as a bonding element. Sit next to a stranger who has also been on a cancer journey and you're family—tied together by shared trauma, tears and triumphs.

Perhaps the best news is that CH works below the level of thinking and therefore is not impacted by brain functioning. There's nothing we need to remember in order for our hearts to grow larger through the experience of a life-altering illness.

This is not to say that CH comes to us automatically or that it can't be distorted by other conditions. Let's be honest, there is a time for the inevitable lament of "Why me?"

The grief that comes with any illness brings with it the inevitable four horsemen of denial, anger, depression and bargaining. CH does not erase these experiences. Instead, it allows us to hold these painful experiences in loving awareness with self-compassion. In the end, CH does not provide an answer to "Why me?" but it can remove the need for the question.

Perhaps, someday they will find a cure (or at least develop preventive techniques) for chemo brain. If we're lucky, there will come a time when everyone is measured by the workings of their hearts rather than their minds and all will see what is truly essential. In that case, we cancer survivors will have a head start.

A Pacifist in the War on Cancer

I am not only a pacifist but a militant pacifist.
I am willing to fight for peace. - Albert Einstein

Recently, I was asked to explain what I meant by identifying myself as a pacifist in the war on cancer. Both my answer and subsequent response from the questioner made me realize that I need to come up with a better explanation.

Let me start by pointing out what being a pacifist in the war on cancer, or PWC, does not mean. It does not mean:

- Staging sit-ins at local oncology offices and telling patients to stop their chemo drugs in favor of herbal remedies.

- Protesting in front of a hospital's radiology department, "Hell no, we won't glow!"

- Refusing medical procedures on the grounds that, "They're not my thing."

- Becoming a welcome mat for the disease.

Most importantly, a PWC does not look down on those who use war metaphors to gather the courage to face cancer.

Being a PWC stands for striving for inner peace and reducing the amount of stress associated with a life-altering illness. It means creating a safe-haven, a sacred space for healing and wellness, rather than a battlefield littered with land mines and hostile encounters at every turn. PWC is really a state of being rather than a state of doing. One can avail oneself to all means necessary to treat cancer, while at the same time adopting an attitude of humility over hostility and compassion over combat.

This is not to suggest that one surrenders, in the normal sense of the word. There is no putting down of arms and admitting defeat. Neither is there retreating to some quickly constructed "happy place" where the real emotions of anger, fear and sadness are masked over with the slippery smile of, "I'm fine." Surrender, in the PWC world, is, as the psychiatrist and author Sheldon Kopp once wrote, to "raise your right hand against fear: extend the other in compassion." It's taking the stand that a war fought within has the self as the first casualty.

Unfortunately, we live in a culture that associates pacifists with cowards. For the most part, I'm OK with that. As someone who struggles with anxiety, when it came to cancer, I was scared to ... well ... life. Fear drove me to ask for the thoughts and prayers of friends, family and strangers. I was afraid to my core that after surviving open heart surgery to remove the thymic tumor growing in my chest, I would not survive the combined hit of radiation and chemo therapies. More to the point, I was terrified that if I declared war on cancer, I would awaken a sleeping giant and rather than emerge as a conqueror enjoying the spoils, end up a refugee trapped in the ravaged landscape of my body.

The other reason that I'm OK with the misconception of pacifism is I know there is something courageous about taking a stand with a plowshare rather than a sword. It takes strength to stay in harmony with life while the body is experiencing a calamity just as throwing oneself into the din of the battle is a hero's/heroine's journey. This journey is shared by all survivors, whether they go to war, or take the stance of a conscientious objector: All deserve Medals of Honor and Purple Hearts. All deserve the end to hostilities.

After the War on Cancer

The supreme art of war is to subdue the
enemy without fighting. - Sun Tzu

I've been waiting anxiously for its arrival ever since I hit the official five-year mark of cancer survival. Every day, I check my mailbox and feverishly sift through bills, junk mail, and more bills, hoping that there will be the golden ticket of all golden tickets: my discharge papers from the war on cancer.

All of us who are called up to the frontlines of the cancer battlefield know that, much like today's military, tours of duty are not set in stone. There is, however, a benchmark that is dangled in front of our weary eyes that has the qualities of both a desert mirage and a whispered promise, "five years ... if you can make it, you're free." Sort of.

While it's true that even saying the c-word is like uttering the name of he-who-must-not-be-named in the Harry Potter saga, it's the other c-word that rarely (if ever) gets mentioned. As a matter of fact, the only time the word *cure* is used in association with cancer is when it is preceded by the words, "your doctor will never use the word ..." Instead, we hear about "survival rates," "remission" and "progression-free." Rather than receiving a congratulatory letter for our service and its termination, we're lucky if we get a hearty handshake and assurance that the odds are in our favor.

Given the unending nature of the war on cancer, many survivors develop something akin to PTSD, only without the *post* and live with "permanent traumatic stress disorder." The antidote for this trauma is to swallow the bitter pill of "there is no cure" and live each day as if it were Armistice — the ending of hostilities — Day. Away from the hum of the radiation machine and the constant drip of the chemo bag, we find the peace of neutrality. Here, we can let down our guard — neither having to fight the disease or the incessant barrage of thoughts that lurk in the shadows — snipers taking aim at our sanity.

It's a fragile peace, to say the least. The smallest little bump, lesion or internal ache can awaken the sleeping giant of fear that lives just across the border of the safe haven we create through the love and support of friends and family. With a stiff upper lip and a quivering lower one, we dare to enjoy this peace and even revel in it. Then it dawns on us that after five years or fifty, cancer will always be our neighbor. We understand the options — we can live in fear, live in hope of a cure, live in denial or simply live.

Whether we choose to carry on as a warrior or lucky survivor, we all went eye-to-eye, toe-to-toe, *mano a mano* with the enemy and were forever changed by the experience. While the medical professionals may never reward our struggles by bestowing the honor of calling us "cured," there comes a time when we appreciate the true meaning of cure which is "care and concern." In this arena, we are all heroes.

How Do You Spell Relief?

Give up the feeling of responsibility, let go your hold, resign the care of your destiny to higher powers ... and you will find not only that you gain a perfect inward relief, but often also, in addition, the particular goods you sincerely thought you were renouncing. - Williams James

In a word, "Whew". Another scan came back negative and I'm positively out of my mind with joy. It's next to impossible to explain the sense of relief that comes from getting this good news, but I'm going to try anyway. It's like being back in Elementary school and the biggest of all bullies tells you, with a menacing look, to meet him on the playground at recess. Then when you arrive, knees knocking, rather than giving you an atomic wedgie, he hands you an ice cream cone, tells you to have a great day, and that he's "got your back" for the rest of the school year. It's like that, only better.

However, in the yin and yang of our world, even this news comes with a reminder that a life lived with humility, gratitude, and even a touch of indifference, makes more sense than living as if we can outsmart the universe.

While sending out the requests for energy, prayers, and good vibes to my army of faithful supporters, I learned that one of them had recently been diagnosed with cancer. He was just starting down that road of uncertainty that cancer survivors know all too well. I immediately felt

[25]

the pull toward the reflexive, "Damn this disease," response. My hands were being drawn to type out some, war on cancer, encouragement. Instead, I was able to corral my fingers and coordinate them to write a more empathetic reply. This particular friend is a kindred spirit, a gentle heart of the highest order, and my ranting about his need to "fight the good fight" would be meaningless.

Knowing full well that there was nothing I could say that would make it all better, I chose the response that seemed to work the best for me in the early days of my illness. I told him that he already has within him all the resources he will need to meet this challenge and to know that when he needs extra those of us who care for him will lend him ours. I then, silently, offered him the Chemo Heart prayer:

Letting go
I am care free
In surrender
I am cared for
In the hands of Life I bear its grief
With an open heart I find relief.

The Triumph of Tragedy

The courage of life is often a less dramatic spectacle than the courage of a final moment; but it is no less a magnificent mixture of triumph and tragedy
- John F. Kennedy

Our culture seems to have the habit of marking time by the occurrence of tragedies. The question "Where were you when . . ?" is meant to point out how powerful the imprint of disasters, natural or man-made, is on the human psyche. The series of traumatic events that make up that list has grown quiet large, even over my own relatively short (relative to human history, that is) life span.

On the positive side, there was the Beatles landing in America, men landing on the moon, the Star Trek series landing on TV, and Cabbage Patch dolls landing in every store in the country. Sadly what, more often, springs to mind are events whose lasting effects were not due to a sense of triumph but a sense of fear, panic, and despair.

People touched by cancer, and other illnesses, have a similar way of marking their personal histories. Very few will ever forget what they were doing when they received their diagnosis. The start of chemotherapy, radiation, and/or surgeries also become memorable benchmarks. Some are so devastated by these events that they will even attach a previous historic marker to the experience. I have heard a number of people refer to their illness as their own 9/11 or Tsunami.

Personally, I try not to mark the passing of time by tragedies. I have to confess, however, that the whole period from 1991 to 1994 is forever etched in my mind as the time that my beloved Buffalo Bills tragically lost four consecutive Super Bowls.

The problem, going back to the cancer experience, is that there are a myriad of traumatic happenings associated with life-altering illnesses. While throwing away the calendar and living without time certainly has its appeal, it makes keeping doctor's appointments even more challenging.

One of the tricks my wife, Kathy, and I came up with was to neutralize the event by refusing to give it more attention than necessary. It is surprising how quickly something will slip from memory when not attached to a mental Post-it Note. Another trick was avoiding telling stories around each new twist and turn. Then there was the blog that I started once I could feel my fingers through the haze of pain meds. Putting our experiences into neat little essays helped to encapsulate the week's events and send them off to the caring energy fields of friends and family members.

The most powerful method for cleansing our calendar was to keep track of, and celebrate, the triumphs. Early on, these were not as easily identifiable and required a little "thinking outside the box." For instance, the day that we were freaked out by the horrific bedside manner of the first surgeon who was scheduled to do my surgery became the glorious, *Day We Chose to Have Thoracic Surgery Somewhere Else*. Later, there were true victories: discharge from the hospital, negative results on the biopsies of lymph nodes, the ending of radiation therapy, the ending of chemotherapy, and the first signs that my hair was not only growing back, it was coming back without the gray.

Marking time with events that buoy the spirit rather than sink it, is a good practice. Let's face it, we live in a world where the tragic not only catches our attention it captures it and holds it hostage. So why not try and about-face, and hold our attention and awareness on the mystery and miracles all around us?

A Round of Applause for Cancer Survivors

*The applause of a single human being is of great
consequence.* – Raymond Hull

In my role as an employee assistance professional, I do a
lot of public speaking in the form of trainings at worksites.
I have developed my personal introduction for these
events to include the fact that I'm a cancer survivor. I do
this for two, admittedly manipulative, reasons, which I
actually share with my audience. The first is that
experience has taught me that when people learn that I
have been through the cancer journey they are nicer to
me on their evaluations at the end of the talk. My guess is
that the thinking goes along these lines: "Well, he did talk
too fast and drifted off topic, but, hey, he survived cancer
— excellent presentation!"

The second reason I share this information is that on
almost every occasion I get a round of applause. At this
point, I will usually comment that it's nice to be
acknowledged for still being alive. I find it a good way to
warm of the crowd and get them on my side, even before I
start the formal talk about whatever workplace topic I'm
addressing. This points to an interesting phenomenon
about this illness; there is a certain celebrity that comes
with being a cancer survivor.

Normally, we only applaud performers, actors, musicians, comedians or athletes as way to show our appreciation for their particular skill. This is our culturally accepted way for thanking someone who has made us feel good. The notable exception to this rule seems to be politicians, who are often applauded out of either respect or to cue them that it's time to stop talking.

This raises the question, "What is it that cancer survivors bring to other people that they feel the need to clap their hands in tribute?" My best guess is that it is a combination of the following factors:

1. Due to the inherent fear in almost everyone about getting cancer, seeing someone who is still around inspires a great sense of hope and they applaud us for being an inspiration.

2. The knowledge that cancer treatment itself can be trauma-inducing and life-threatening creates a deeps sense of respect and they applaud our courage.

3. It's about a close to meeting someone who has come back from the dead as most people will ever get and they applaud our celebrity-like status.

The experience of standing in front of complete strangers, who are clapping and celebrating ('celebrate' being one of the origins of the word celebrity) is so pleasant and comforting that I think that we need to make it a routine part of cancer treatment. How about a round of applause every time we sit in the chemotherapy chair or lie down on the radiation table? How about a rousing dose of it whenever we show up for our regular scans, blood work and X-rays? Finally, how about a victory lap around the oncologists office when we meet cancer survivor milestones?

Anyone who has ever been a part of a Relay for Life event knows the smiles that show up when we take our victory lap to the cheers of loved ones and other survivors. We also know that it's not the applause itself but the loving energy, care and concern that allows us to celebrate — to assemble to honor — a life lived with cancer. To those who do not have the opportunity to share their survivorship with a cheering crowd, know that I offer you a standing ovation and, in my eyes, you are all rock stars worthy of an encore.

Cancer as Yoga

This attitude of silent observation is the very foundation of yoga.–Sri Nisargaddata Maharaj

During a recent counseling session, a client was sharing with me the current stressors in his life. He was feeling increasing pressure both at home and at work and it was exacting a heavy toll on his overall health. At some point during our talk he mentioned that he is a cancer survivor, having been through treatment, recurrence, and a second treatment. He proudly pointed to the scar on his chest where his port had been and talked about what it was like to see a "dying face in the mirror everyday" only to find the courage to face another round of chemotherapy.

As I listened, recalling my own scars from the cancer trek, he hit upon a theme that I have found in many of the people I've worked with who've been through life-altering experiences. This theme, which I have to confess I find within myself, he expressed as "I can't believe I'm letting these little things in life bother me again."

I've often heard from people who've gone through traumatic experiences that their perspectives shifted and revealed previously unknown qualities. The self that each discovered was more resilient, courageous and balanced. Upon reflection, many see this as one of the gifts that come from living with an uncertain future. The eventual return to the more familiar self, filled with worries, lacking in self-confidence and a victim of past and future, is what I refer to as the persistence of personality. This was crystallized for me by a young woman who had been through treatment for breast cancer who said, "I was a better person while going through treatment."

The fact that the shock of a cancer diagnosis and the journey into the labyrinth of treatment, can bring about dramatic shifts in one's self has deep roots in psychology. It can even be said that the primary aim of psychotherapy is to help facilitate such transformations. That these changes often don't become permanent is a testament to the strength of our egoic selves — the mind-made sense of who we are — and the habitual manner in which most of us live our lives.

The great news for anyone who has had this experience and now laments the loss of the "Now I see what's important" self, is that it is not lost. The even greater news is that, rather than a temporary response, arising momentarily out of chaos, it is, in fact, our true nature. It is the shattering impact of a cancer diagnosis that shakes the foundations of the ego and cracks its hard shell. Through these cracks emerges the ever-present, shining, true self.

For many of us survivors, the further we move away from the treatment experience, the less contact we seem to have with the "better person." Looking at the world again through old eyes, molehills once again become mountains, it rains on every parade and our fantasy football picks are hurt on the first play from scrimmage; life starts to hurt again. At this point, some survivors will practice the mantra of "I've been through worse." While certainly true, this chant seldom works for very long as memory is never as powerful as our here-and-now experience.

In my work as a therapist, a leader of a cancer support group and seven years into my own survivorship, I find the middle path works the best when it comes to the persistence of personality. When working with clients I will suggest that they see the return of their old patterns of thinking and behaving as a natural rebound effect. It is the ego's job to try to maintain a sense of familiarity, to include our idiosyncrasies and dysfunctional behaviors. I try to help them see that this self only grows stronger when they resist and try to fight. I will then remind them that their true selves emerged during their time of crisis not due to their effort, but to surrender. It was there in

[37]

the shadows just waiting for the moment when their attempts to control life failed.

Upon further investigation, we understand that it was not the cancer that brought about these changes (good news for those who want the experience without the illness), it was the shift into a level of present moment awareness we seldom allow ourselves.

When we no longer live in a remembered past and imagined future we experience what Eckhart Tolle has called, "the power of now." In this state, fears, worries and anxieties are transmuted into peace. In this way, cancer itself becomes yoga; a joining the outer self, with its habitual patterns of fight and flight, with the inner self and its reflexive response of equanimity. The timeless act of dividing the world, if even just for a moment, ends and duality merges into the absolute oneness.

F.E.A.R. Factor

Perhaps everything that frightens us is, in its deepest essence, something helpless that wants our love.
-Rainer Maria Rilke

If there is one thing that all cancers have in common, it's fear. Whether it is the fear of a known, of the unknown, of loss, or fear of pain and suffering — fear is one of the primary symptoms of this diagnosis.

I have to confess that when it comes to fear, I have lived with its annoying offspring, anxiety, most of my life. For the uninitiated, anxiety, in its purest form, is like having to sit through a horror movie. The movie is your life, though, and the monsters, ghosts and zombies exist only in your head. My more clinical description for anxiety, the one that I share with clients who also carry the same freak-out potential, is that anxiety is when we worry about our worries.

"Everyone's afraid of something," I tell them, "those of us who are anxious have the extra fear of the worrisome thoughts themselves."

It was during a particularly intense and extended episode of anxiety several years ago that I was beaten up to the point of exhaustion. Traditional methods of calming my mind did not work, so I decided that there had to be another way to manage the experience. This started me down the path of meditation and the practice of mindfulness.

Contrary to much of what I was taught in my training as a psychotherapist, mindfulness practitioners were saying that it is the attempt to avoid the very things that scare us that creates our suffering. This seemed counterintuitive at first. Why would I not want to fight my anxiety? It was making my life miserable. What I wanted was a book called "Kick Anxiety's Ass: 10 Way to Achieve Peace of Mind."

It wasn't long, however, before the wisdom of the mindfulness practice of accepting the present moment, without judging or wishing it to be other than it is, began to payoff. The mindfulness axiom of "Whatever we resist persists" made perfect sense to me, as it seemed that my attempts not to be anxious only made me more anxious.

What I didn't know at the time was that my year of living anxiously was actually preparing me for the challenges I would face when diagnosed with cancer. The mindfulness techniques that I picked up during this period were essential to not letting the, "What next?" train run me over. The ability to step back from the thinking mind and stay in the now helped me to further understand that the only thing I had to fear was the fear of fear itself.

This is not to say that I was not afraid of having cancer, or that chemotherapy was going to make me sick and bald, and, of course, I was afraid I would glow like a nightlight after radiation therapy.

The fears associated with any life-altering illness are endless. Fortunately, mindfulness practices taught me to find comfort in facing those fears, not with a sword in hand ever at the ready to slay the beast, but by, as the writer Sheldon Kopp once advised, "... raising my right hand against fear and extending the other in compassion."

This practice helped me to look within during times that I was most afraid. The timeless promise of this ancient practice is the realization that, in the words of the poet Rilke, "We have no reason to harbor any mistrust against our world, for it is not against us. If it has terrors, they are our terrors; if it has abysses, these abysses belong to us."

Through both my anxiety and cancer experiences I have learned to extend compassion to that part of me that feels so terrified, that would repeatedly say, especially during chemotherapy, "I can't do this anymore." The mind trick I came up with at the time was to convert fear into FEAR: Face, Embrace, Accept, and Release. During these times, I would hear Rilke's soothing words in my head, "If an anxiety, like light and cloud-shadows, moves over your hands and everything you do, you must realize that something is happening to you, that life has not forgotten you, that it holds you in its hand and will not let you fall."

Facing fear, rather than running the other way, brings one to a turning point in life; courage does not come before we face our worst fears, it comes from the very act of facing them. Embracing fear is not the same a loving the terrible things that are happening to us. It means having compassion for that part in us that feels so afraid, while still being willing to hold the moment in our awareness.

When we allow the moment to be as it is, without resisting or judging, a release comes from a very deep place. With this release the knots of stress, tension and anxiety, unwind themselves. This is the prize for walking through the doorway of fear, or, in my case, tiptoeing through — just in case it was a trap.

When Oncology Becomes Primary

We are all precancerous. – George Carlin

When I walked out of my last radiation session seven years ago, the therapist who shepherded me through the previous 29 pushed play on the boom box and the song, "Hit the Road Jack," filled the air. With smiles, hugs and tears, we said goodbye and the refrain, "don't cha come back no more," couldn't have been more on point.

There was no similar ceremony at the oncologist's office after the termination of chemotherapy, as the message was clearly delivered, "We are your doctors now, and we will continue to follow your care."

The idea of trading in a primary care physician for an oncologist still brings a knot to my stomach. I'm well aware that the biannual blood tests and annual X-rays have one purpose: scanning for the return of the monster. As a result, I always feel strange sitting in the waiting room of my oncologist's office.

Seven years out, I can still recall the feeling of being in active treatment, waiting for my name to be called so I could take my chair and get hooked up for the next five hours. I cannot help but scan the room these days and feel deep empathy for those who I know are only starting their journey. At times, I feel a twinge of survivor's guilt as I sit with my regrown hair, full blood count and absence of chemo-induced fatigue. During these times, I remember what it felt like to be starting this challenge and how I felt when survivors showed up, aglow with a radiance that comes from having survived the perfect storm of physical and emotional traumas. To ease this guilt, I imagine that I'm being seen as an inspiration — living proof, with a huge emphasis on the living part — that treatment can work, the beast can be tamed. However, part of me is aware that others may be thinking, as I did on occasion, "How dare you look so healthy!"

The sobering moment arrives when I see that person who I know may never get to have a final appointment, who may never know the relief of a clear CT scan or blood work. To say that one is humbled by this awareness falls short of the affective response deep within one's heart. As a professional healer, I want to reach out and hold that person's deepest fears while they regain, if even for a moment, the ability to breathe freely again. I want to tell them that I know the demons they face and assure them that, despite how it appears, all is well

Instead of opening up my therapist tool kit, however, I choose to sit as a silent patient who's simply waiting his

[44]

turn to be called to see the doctor. Often, I recite a silent prayer or healing mantra to the others who wait with me, as there are moments when no words can be just as powerful as any cliché: "Hang in there," or "It will get better."

When I walk out of the doctor's office, I pass a renal clinic, a gastroenterology department and outpatient surgical practice. I see old and young, fit and feeble, walking or being wheeled, to their next destination and am struck by a sense of kinship. Sure, we're all connected at that moment by the label "patient," but it's a deeper connection one senses; a communal sharing of the fragility, humility and resiliency of the human spirit. While I still hate having an oncologist as my PCP, tempered by this experience of community, it's a hate I hope to have well into the future.

Refueling the Caregiver

Doctors diagnose, nurses heal, and Caregivers
make sense of it all. — Brett H. Lewis

Through my practice as a psychotherapist, and my role as a caregiver support group leader, I've met many people who described an experience that I've only recently been able to name. This experience, which I witnessed first-hand when my wife took on the caregiver role during my cancer treatment, has to do with two essential life forces operating at the same time.

The word that came to mind as I watched my wife shift into caregiver mode was "exhaustlessness" — being both fatigued and restless at the same time. I realize now that this is what I see on the faces of the caregivers who come to me for professional guidance. It is the look that says, "There's so much to do and so little time to do it that the only thing I can do is keep moving."

The physical manifestation is like taking a sleeping pill and an energy drink at the same time. One is always "on-call" and those cherished moments of rest seek to replenish physical, mental, emotional and spiritual energies.

[47]

Exhaustlessness is the perfect stress storm — the collision of two powerful systems whose combined impact can feel like an emotional hurricane. Under different circumstances, facing this flood of circumstances would leave one depleted and despondent. Paradoxically, exhaustlessness becomes the very fuel that energizes the caregiver. It provides the wherewithal to sit through countless appointments, manage multiple priorities like a circus juggler and fend off sleep as one sits bedside, ever watchful of a loved one's every move, despite eyes that are heavy as the heart.

The reason that exhaustlessness does not come with the Surgeon General's warning of "dangerous to your health" is, I believe, due to it arising out of a movement of profound love. While caring for others runs the risk of burnout when the awareness of personal limits is ignored, heart-centered exhaustlessness provides a return on the investment. Through the act of selfless compassion, the illusion of separation dissolves—the giver and receiver are one and you get what you give.

This exchange of energy explains why it's hard to convince caregivers to slow down, and why they often look sideways at anyone who tells them that they have to take care of themselves first. At a very deep level, the level where we're all connected, they are taking care of themselves as they move reflexively toward the needs of a

[48]

loved one who is suffering. The well that feeds this energy is unlimited, which is why many caregivers seem to perform miracles in their acts of service.

Like many of those who've faced the cancer challenge with a loved one as their caregiver, I've often thought that my wife's role was even more difficult than mine. I had a team of professionals looking after me, the latest medications to manage side effects and the prayers and healing energies of extended family members, friends and colleagues. My wife, on the other hand, was often flying solo, without a treatment plan, pills to manage the ups and downs, or someone to take the next shift when her patient (yours truly) was in a foul mood. What she did have, however, was a love that soothed the radiation burns, countered the chemo-induced fatigue, calmed the steroid-fueled rants and even, without any sense of falseness, verbalized, "You really look good without hair."

Given my personal experience, I'm no longer surprised that many of the caregivers I see are not looking for permission to stop, but confirmation that it's OK to continue. Increasingly, I find myself helping them see the forces at work within themselves and move in accord with their inner wisdom. Finally, I ask that they allow trusted others to shoulder some of the burdens that come with caregiving and assure them that, while the experience of exhaustlessness will pass, the love remains forever.

Healing on a Wing and a Prayer

If we only pray or meditate when we are in perfect health, we will never be able to produce peace and joy. We have to sign a peace treaty so that we can live in peace with our ill health. - Thich Nhat Hanh

As a pacifist in the war on cancer, I'm not one to use battle analogies when describing the challenges of this diagnosis. The one expression, however, that I think is befitting is, "There are no atheists in foxholes." The obvious explanation for this is that when sitting on the edge of life or death, not only does one believe there is a God, one begins a running dialogue with this higher power; a dialogue commonly known as prayer.

According to a recent CDC study, 69 percent of cancer patients say they pray for their health. If I had to guess, I would say the other 31 percent are doing the same thing but just call it something else. The study also reveals that, "... people who found feelings of transcendence or meaningfulness or peace reported feeling the least physical problems."

Therefore, a common expression could be, "There are no nonbelievers in the chemo rooms." This speaks volumes of the connection between spirituality and surviving tough times.

Later on in the article, spirituality is defined as, "A connection to a force larger than oneself." While many people feel the need to name this "force," its name is not nearly as important as what it represents — even that pales in comparison to what it can provide those who are facing life's big questions.

During my own treatment, I went with the more-is-better philosophy and connected with as many possible sources of a higher power as I could get my nervously shaking hands on. The list included prayer, yoga, meditation, qi gong, aromatherapy, reiki, bio-energy healing, pranayama and mantras. Being able to draw from this potpourri of options greatly affected my everyday experience, not only of my cancer treatment, but my life as a whole.

When I meet others (in my work as a therapist) who are going through health crises, I will often introduce the topic of spirituality. Knowing that this can be a warning sign to some clients that they have stumbled into a counselor's office who is going to try to convert them, I reassure them that this topic has been researched and proven to impact their overall well-being. Almost everyone I've met has gone on to talk freely about his or her beliefs and how they are helping — or, at times, hindering — their attempts to cope with the crisis.

People's reaction to their spiritual nature during challenging times fascinates me, and I will always share my own if it seems appropriate for the client. Many people have told me that they've leaned heavily on their personal understanding of God and have, in fact, prayed for healing. This always takes me back to my own private moments, surrounded by the dark unknown, trying to compose the perfect prayer.

Unless my chemo brain is playing tricks on me, I can say that I never prayed to have my cancer taken away. This is due, mostly, to my career as an anxious person who did not want to have to face the challenge of figuring out what an answer of "no" meant. Instead, I used various practices to calm my wandering mind, short-circuit the stress response, implant the intention to live a life of wellness, and restore a balance between my body and mind. If there was a go-to prayer, it was some version of, "give me the strength to get through this moment."

Despite doubts, fears and emotional breakdowns, I found this prayer was always answered.

Prayer helps us heal whether we believe in a spiritual realm or not. No single religious faith, dogma, or belief system can lay claim to being the "it" factor when it comes to this healing power. As a student of Eastern philosophies, and a Reiki practitioner, I believe in energy systems and their direct connection to both illness and wellness. As someone brought up in the Christian faith, I also believe in following the guidance of sages, prophets and saints. However we frame our understanding of spirituality, and to whomever or whatever we pray, I believe it is the willingness to let go of our will and rest in the present moment that provides what is needed.

That it often takes a health crisis, or other traumatic life event, to direct our attention to the spiritual realm, should give us pause to reflect on the deeper meaning of illness. It should be no surprise that many cancer patients report awakening to "what's really important" as a result of their diagnosis.

The Buddhist peace activist Thich Nhat Hanh tells us that we should embrace our illness in the same way we embrace our wellness, and find meaning in our suffering. Jesus said, "Pick up your cross and follow me," and the psychologist Carl Jung said there is no birth of consciousness without pain. If cancer, or any other illness, can help us transmute our suffering into peace, our sorry into joy, then I say "Amen" to that.

Happy Holidays?

The holiest of holidays are those kept by ourselves in silence and apart; the secret anniversaries of the heart.
-Henry Wadsworth Longfellow

Seven years ago, I was ready to jump on the holiday stress sleigh and then I was diagnosed with cancer one week after Thanksgiving. I still remember that Christmas, as my wife and I awaited the thoracic surgery that was going to remove the tumor growing in my chest. Knowing that after surgery, chemo and radiation therapies were waiting in the wings, there was little holiday spirit in the air. There was, however, a strange peace.

Upon reflection, it occurred to us that as a result of challenges ahead of us, the usual holiday madness was not stressing us out. There were no concerns about parties to attend or not attend, no worries about finances to cover the costs of gifts, no fears of family functions becoming dysfunctional — none of the usual seasonal stressors.

One of the gifts that can come from a life-altering illness is the release of needless worries. Away from the mind wanderings of "what if," there is a space where all is quiet, all is calm. Whether this inner peace comes from a meditative practice or simply being fully awake to the present moment, the silent mind becomes a whole mind and we no longer feel like we're going to pieces.

Don't get me wrong, the holidays still get hectic. However, the stress does not feel the same. I find it helpful to see this time of year as the beginning of my survivorship. Whenever I feel my inner Grinch getting ready to make an appearance, I think back to where I was seven years ago and the fact that my online shopping cart just crashed doesn't seem like such a catastrophe.

Realizing that not everyone has had a holiday epiphany and many more are facing the beginning of their cancer challenges, I wrote the following Stressmas carols as reminders of the true spirit of the season.

Jangled Nerves (sung to the tune of Jingle Bells)

Oh, jangled nerves, jangled nerves
Jangled all the day
Oh how sad it is to spend
Our holiday time this way
Dashing through the malls
With a cart that's gone astray
Back to the bank we go
Crying all the way

Bells on registers ring
Making spirits sigh
Oh, what bills the mailman brings
Why is my interest rate so high?
Oh, jangled nerves, jangled nerves
Jangled all the day
Oh how sad it is to spend
Our holiday time this way
A day or two ago
I felt my chest grow tight
And very soon I found myself
Pacing through the night
I tried to get some sleep
But the fears they would not go
I knew I'd fallen very deep
I never felt so low
Oh, jangled nerves, jangled nerves
Jangled all the day
Oh how sad it is to spend
Our holiday time this way

Let It Go (sung to the tune of Let It Snow)

Oh, the world outside if frightful
And everyone seems so spiteful
But since it's no way to grow
I let it go, let it go, let it go

[57]

The stress it is not stoppin'
And my heart it feels like poppin'
But before I hit an all-time low
I let it go, let it go, let it go
And when I finally see the light
Nothing seems quite so bad
When I surrender to the fight
I discover the peace that I had
Now the fears are slowly dying
And my hearts no longer crying
All I ever needed to know
Was let it go, let it go, let it go

The Healing Power of Pets

*An animal's eyes have the power to speak
a great language. - Martin Buber*

On the day that I bit the bullet and shaved off the hair that was quickly abandoning my scalp due to chemotherapy, I had my picture taken with our Great Dane, Daphne. I did this because I always feel better around our pets, no matter what's happening. Additionally, I knew that I would be sending the picture to friends and family and her presence would soften the shock of my new look.

As an animal lover and psychotherapist, I've seen the healing power of pet therapy firsthand. From horses to dogs, cats and rabbits, the impact that animals have on recovery is nothing short of miraculous. Therefore, I think that everyone who receives a diagnosis of cancer should also receive a puppy (or other small animal of their liking) right after they're advised about the possible side effects that can come with chemotherapy.

According to the Cancer Treatment Centers of America, pets provide the following benefits to those going through cancer treatment:

- Easing their anxiety and elevating their mood

- Offering company and comfort, thereby lessening feelings of isolation or loneliness

- Providing a distraction from pain, stress or boredom

- Relaxing them, especially since petting or snuggling with a soft, friendly animal can release endorphins that have a calming effect

- Motivating them to get better

- Increasing socialization and encouraging communication

All of these great benefits and the only side effect is occasionally being slobbered on.

To anyone who is already a pet owner, it's old news that pets help keep us healthy and sane. Those of us who've routinely shared our homes with pets don't need scientific data to prove that the animals we invite into our lives occupy a special place in our hearts.

Aside from the Internet sensation of cat and kitten videos, pets provide much more than just entertainment. From companionship to unqualified acceptance, pets should be on the top of anyone's wellness checklist. I've heard from numerous clients experiencing physical and/or mental distress that their pets were keeping them grounded.

Personally, my daily walks with our dogs were an important ritual that provided a sense of normalcy to days where nothing made sense. I knew that when I came home, under the heavy burden of thinking, "I can't do this anymore," our Brittany, Sage, would meet me at the door, favorite squeaky toy in her mouth, with a look that said, "Yes you can, now let's play fetch."

One of the more powerful (yet overlooked) aspects of having pets around during recovery is that they allow those of us who are in the care-receiving category to reach out and care for something beyond ourselves. This extension of loving energy has a rebound effect as we gain the awareness that, in spite of our illness, we have much to offer. I found that our cats' purrs of appreciation would drown out the echoes of the radiation machine like a meditative mantra easing me toward peaceful rest.

Naysayers would suggest that we animal lovers simply project human qualities onto our pets. To them I say, "Try telling that to my 110-pound Great Dane and she'll bite your knees off!" (Actually, like her dad, she's more of a pacifist and prefers napping over nipping).

What connects us to our furry friends is not that we project human qualities onto them; they bring out the true humanity in us. In addition, without the human ego, animals are more connected to the source of life and therefore offer a portal to the present moment. In the wonderful book "Guardians of Being," Eckhart Tolle writes,

[61]

"It's so wonderful to watch an animal, because it has no opinion about itself."

Rather than make them more like us, we would all do better with a more dog-like philosophy of "sit, stay and heel" as an antidote to all of our frantic wanderings.

I still remember with fondness an in-home counseling session I had years ago with an elderly gentleman who had recently lost his wife. He had been struggling with depression since that time and found it hard to look after his health. While he talked with me, his golden retriever sat quietly at his feet. With both sadness and gratitude, he pointed out that they had brought the dog home while his wife was still ill. Looking back at it, he said he realized that she'd done it for him, so that he would not be alone when she was gone. Understanding the profound comfort being provided, I simply petted the dog and agreed that it was a truly loving act and more help than my counseling could provide. I knew he was in good hands — or to be more accurate — paws.

The Gratitude Attitude

Gratitude bestows reverence, allowing us to encounter everyday epiphanies, those transcendent moments of awe that change forever how we experience life and the world.
- John Milton

The poet Rumi once wrote, "Wear gratitude like a cloak and it will feed every corner of your life."

I put this cloak on the day I was diagnosed with cancer and I have to say that not only did it fit like a well-worn garment, I looked good in it. When wearing it, the important things in life seemed to spring up all around me. What once only occupied a small corner of my field of vision became the background against which all of life's happenings were cast. Mindless moments spent waiting became meditations of solitude, helping to dissolve stress.

In gratitude, no stone was left unturned as even passing encounters with strangers became opportunities to reconnect with everyday life beyond a cancer diagnosis. The simple things transformed into essential reminders of the delicate and intricate wonder of life.

I would like to say that I've worn this cloak since that day, however the truth is, more frequently than I like to admit, it goes back into the closet. During these times, I once again sweat the small stuff; petty annoyances unnerve me, my fuse grows shorter, and I yell at traffic, as if my travel needs should be everyone's concern. Minus the framework of thankfulness, epiphanies give way to confusion, awe turns to fear and wonder gives way to questioning the point of it all.

This time of year, one of the traditions that coincides with resolutions, is the reflection on what I have to be thankful for. This experience can be challenging. In my personal and professional talks with other cancer survivors, they often describe an experience that I've come to know all too well.

This experience can be summed up as, "Cancer made me appreciate the people and things in my life more than ever, but now I can't seem to stop taking them for granted."

The question that often follows is some form of, "Why can't I just be grateful all the time?"

My therapeutic answer to the question is this: "Life happened. Sometimes life hurts, and it's hard to be thankful while in pain."

So as not to leave someone feeling as if I just handed him or her the parental nugget of, "Life's not fair, so suck it up," I will point out the following observations that came to me through the cancer journey:

1. Cancer doesn't make us see what's meaningful; we see it when our attention turns away from the minutia and trivial distractions that surround us.

2. We don't ever lose our appreciation, but we can misplace it.

3. Taking life for granted is essentially our culturally-induced default mode — we are trained to overlook the essential.

4. Being thankful is a habit that grows stronger the more we engage in it.

5. It's OK if, in the moment, the only thing we can think of to be grateful for is the fact that we're aware that we're not being very appreciative.

Trial and error has taught me that the best response to someone who's struggling to complete his or her gratitude list is, "I know what that struggle feels like."

I save the speeches on how we know, through psychological research, that gratitude is good medicine. I will not preach about the physiological impact that holding thankful thoughts has on the heart. I know from my own experience, being *told* to be thankful, rings hollow and the look that ensues is often that of a little child who's been scolded for not being more grateful.

As I look back on another year of survivorship and the approach of the seventh anniversary of my surgery, I've come to the realization that my cloak of gratitude is always in fashion. While I may not experience Milton's, "transcendent moments of awe," while wearing it, I am reminded of what's important.

For that, I'm very grateful.

Bedside Manners

It is not a case we are treating; it is a living, palpitating, alas, too often suffering fellow creature. - John Brown

A 2015 article in U.S. News magazine had the following heading, Why Nice Doctors Are Better Doctors: *A good bedside manner could mean the difference between illness and health.* The gist of the piece was that, "Your doctor's empathy, or the ability to stand in your shoes, not only deepens the relationship between the two of you and makes you feel more satisfied with your visit, but also has measurable effects on your health." As a psychotherapist trained in the arts of empathy, listening and unconditional positive regard, and a survivor of cancer, I would like to add a professional, "No, duh!"

After clearing the initial hurdles of discovery, diagnosis, surgery, chemo and radiation therapies, I considered penning a work entitled "Who Cares?" The book was going to be a summation of the things I heard and experienced over the months of recovery that, frankly, freaked me out. I decided against the effort for two reasons; the first being that my oncologist and his team were professional, caring and sensitive to my needs and I didn't want to be seen as ungrateful. The second reason I held off was that I was not ready to relive all the interactions I had with other health providers where that was not the case.

Seven years removed from the experience and goaded on by the tales of other patients who've suffered the added insult of poor professional behavior, I now feel it's time to point out the obvious. Surely, I'm not the first person to take note of the fact that the second word in the title of health care professional is, in fact, *care*.

My guess is that every cancer survivor has his or her own list of negative interactions that took place while in treatment. Some may have even said something to address and/or correct the situation. However, many (like me) were too knocked down by the diagnosis to stand up for their right to be treated with respect and dignity.

The following is a true story:

My wife and I arrived at a local university hospital to await my appointment with the surgeon scheduled to perform the thoracic surgery to remove the tumor growing in my chest. Checking in at the reception desk, we were given a number and told we would be called back in short order. Let me restate that, we were given a number!

Waiting nervously, we exchanged multiple jokes about being at the deli counter. Once called back, we were greeted by a physician's assistant who seemed to grasp the enormity of the moment and did her best, it's-going-to-be-OK interview. Next, the surgeon joined us and, with absolutely no sense of anything, placed the tip of his index finger at the top of my chest and drawing it down to my sternum said, "We're going to cut from here to here and," drawing an arc over the tip of my left chest, "remove this part of your lung."

I remember very little from that point on as his next statement was that my type of cancer was often related to testicular cancer. Without so much of a "How do you do?" he proceeded with the exam, surrounded by a bevy of interns, all of whom were, no doubt, impressed with his laser-like focus on my family jewels. Angry, shocked and bewildered, my wife and I left the appointment and made two very important decisions. The first was that, at some point in the future, we were both going to laugh about this and that there was no way I was going under this guy's knife.

I wish I could say that the above anecdote was the one and only time we ran into a situation where we were alarmed — rather than calmed — by a medical encounter. From a casual disregard for my anxiety in the face of this dreaded illness, to the blatant lack of compassion, the number of times we ran into trained professionals who seemed oblivious to the person behind the patient was disheartening.

I've heard stories about how a health care provider has an awakening after he or she becomes a patient and discovers first-hand the negative impact of poor bedside manners. While these stories always spark interest, they are a sad commentary on what is, too often, taken for granted in the medical profession — there are people attached to diagnoses. One has to ask if professionals really needs to have a health crisis in order to understand that the first instrument in their medical bags is their attitude.

Personally, I'm not asking them to "feel my pain," but it's comforting to see some awareness of my suffering. I'm not talking about the overcorrection of the Patch Adams effect. Honestly, I don't want my doctor coming at me with a red nose and clown shoes. I would like, however, if he or she approached me in ways that do not make me look or feel foolish for having the audacity to expect to be treated with consideration.

Imagine not having to choose between a person's technical skill and their compassion. Imagine being able to keep one's dignity after putting on the inherently humiliating garment known as a hospital gown. I suggest that right under the obligatory signs that remind health care workers to practice universal precautions while seeing a patient, we add a line that reminds them to engage in the universally accepted practice of good manners. In that way, we can stay safe from infections, while at the same time avoid contact with toxic attitudes that are dangerous to our health.

Surviving Survivor's Guilt

There's no problem so awful that you can't add some guilt to it and make it even worse. - Bill Watterson: *The Complete Calvin and Hobbes*

Why me? Cancer survivors have an interesting relationship with these two words. As bookends to the cancer experience, their implications and impact are crucial to understanding the psychology of a life-threatening illness.

Even the most stoic among us must have at some point allowed the question "Why me?" to cross his or her lips or mind. Not only is it normal to question the arrival of such a traumatic event, it is the reflexive response of a mind honed for survival. I've found that resisting the urge to ask this inevitable question causes more problems than it solves. As a cathartic exercise, shouting to the heavens with a fist shaking, wanting to know the point of it all, helps to clear the way for a more heart-centered approach to healing.

At the other end of the cancer continuum, "Why me?" takes on tones of irony, empathy and longing. When the element of having done something wrong is added to the

[73]

questioning of one's survival, we end up with survivor's guilt. Here, the struggle is not coming to terms with illness, but an existential wrestling match with the meaning of life. Under normal circumstances, this quest for understanding would be both noble and liberating. That survivor's guilt is lumped into the category of "things I can live without" speaks to the corrosive nature of this self-shaming activity that often has very deep roots.

The origin of the word guilt means, crime, sin, moral defect or failure of duty. There are those who contend that guilt (in small doses) can actually serve as a self-correcting mechanism when one's moral compass no longer points to true north — the self-punishment seldom fits the crime. Left unchecked, self-correction becomes self-condemnation that opens the floodgates of depression.

When the question "Why did I get cancer?" becomes "Why did I survive cancer, while others did not?" the guilt reflex is turned on its head. What is there to feel guilty about? No offense has been committed, no moral code broken and no failure of duty took place. How does the victim become a perpetrator? What purpose is served by calling into question the right to awaken to yet another day?

I've learned through trial and error that trying to absolve one of guilt requires more than simply telling the person they have no reason to feel guilty. Ironically, efforts to make a person feel better about being a survivor often leads to an increased sense of shame for not appreciating the gift one has been given.

When I work with survivor's guilt in clinical practice, I introduce my three-step model for surviving survivor's guilt:

Step 1 is to **name it**: Guilt of any type is — more often than not — an echo of someone else's voice. By asking clients to give a name to the guilt trip they're on, they're released from feeling that it is the result of some personal character flaw.

Step 2 is to **claim it**: Owning the times when we're victimizing ourselves with the guilt experience is much easier than trying to ignore, resist and fight. Subtract the feeling that one has failed to rid oneself of this experience and there is no longer the need to feel guilty about feeling guilty.

Step 3 is to **reframe it**: Reframing is a powerful psychological technique that has its roots in the age-old transformation of lemons into lemonade. Once we cast a painful experience in a more positive light, we drain it of its power. Ultimately, survivor's guilt arises from compassion for others and the desire to end suffering.

Finally, I will point out that survivor's guilt can have a bright side. In an attempt to scratch the guilt itch, many people go on to take on causes, donate to charities, seek cures, and, yes, even write blogs. As someone who experiences this phenomenon every time I show up at my oncologist's office for my follow-up visits, my personal mantra is: "I survived cancer, and I'm guilty of wanting the same for others."

Cancer Patience: A Meditation on Waiting

They also serve who only stand and wait. - John Milton

If you're a cancer survivor you've probably spent a good portion of your time waiting. I don't mean waiting for the bus, waiting for the rain to stop or waiting for something good to turn up on Pay-Per-View. The kind of waiting I'm talking about is the gut wrenching, soul squeezing, the-doctor-will-be-with-you-in-a-minute waiting that anyone with a serious illness knows all too well.

This isn't a rant about the medical profession and its apparent twisted sense of time. I want to talk about the psychological nature of waiting itself. The word 'waiting' actually means "to watch over" or simply "watch." This seems relatively harmless and even somewhat quaint, as in, "I think I'll watch to see if those clouds are ever going away."

The problem, of course, comes from the time-addicted mind and its need to keep things moving. Waiting is to the mind what being stranded on the beach is to a fish; a mind thrown into idleness flaps around grasping for something to worry about.

The smorgasbord of waiting that is laid out before you when diagnosed with cancer would be farcical if it were not so physically, psychologically and emotionally draining. Six weeks passed from the time of my diagnosis to the time of surgery. There was the waiting for procedures to done, test results to return, drugs to wear off, drugs to kick in, phone calls to be returned, hair to fall out, hair to grow back, etc. If it was a competition, cancers survivors would continually grab the gold medal in waiting.

One method of dealing with the sense that time is standing still is the time-honored tradition of complaining — also known as being an *impatient patient*. While losing one's cool seems like a good idea, it seldom has the desired effect. The inner tension that builds is simply one more form of stress that the body has to confront. The externalization of that stress on some poor soul (who has seen one too many meltdowns) simply earns one the extra notation, "Mr. Verano is not handling his recovery very well." Believe me; no one waits longer than the one tagged with the asterisk, "Needs to practice being more patient."

The fact that word 'patient' applies to both our role as a receiver of medical services and how we are asked to be while waiting is a sublime irony. The word patience derives from Latin, *patientem*, meaning, "bearing, supporting, suffering, enduring, and permitting."

To put a fine point on it: to be "patiently waiting" is to watch our suffering. No wonder we don't want to get good at it. Fortunately, the observing of the human condition is the very core of meditative practices and opens the door to the transformation of these otherwise exhaustive experiences.

My wife and I chose this meditative path when it came to downtime. Now, don't imagine some New Age couple sitting in lotus position in the oncology office chanting, "om." Instead, we returned to waiting's origin and simply watched. We watched our breathing, our thoughts and the ebb and flow of inner energies. In this way, our waiting became our practice; an invitation to meet ourselves in the present moment. In those 'now' moments, a sense of calm replaced nervous nail biting and the awareness of breath became the awareness of life.

Research has demonstrated the powerful benefits of meditation and mindful attention to the present moment on health and wellness. The essential element is to develop opportunities for stillness. Why not transmute the lead of anxious waiting into the gold of a meditative moment? Why not make the practice of patience one of the silver linings of around the dark cloud of our cancer experience?

The best news of all about dropping in on the present moment is that it's always now, which means (you guessed it): No waiting. Here are some tips for becoming what — in Zen circles — is known as the "silent witness":

1. Tune out the noises around you and tune into your breath. Don't judge it, just watch and see if you notice where in the body you experience it the most.

[79]

2. Give an overly active mind a mantra to silently say over and over. This can be anything meaningful to you, or a simple distraction, e.g. "Watching not waiting, watching not waiting."

3. Use a calming scent. Your sense of smell can trigger the relaxation response at a deeper level than most of the other senses. Some helpful scents include lavender, frankincense and sandalwood. But hey, if the smell of fresh baked bread does it for you, go for it.

4. Give your hands something to do. The deep connection between the body and the mind means that we can influence our mental state through body movement. Worry beads, rosaries, stress balls and even tapping fingers in sequence are good ways to send "calm down" signals to the brain.

5. Forget trying to stop thinking, this only creates further tension. When the thoughts return, watch them and then return to the breath. Repeat as often as needed.

On Hope and Cancer

Hope is the thing with feathers
That perches in the soul,
And sings the tune without the words,
And never stops at all
-Emily Dickinson

I was doing some, pre-spring, cleaning recently and came across the t-shirt from my first Relay for Life. The event took place on June 6, 2010, the day after my last chemotherapy session. It was a typical southern Virginia afternoon where the heat and humidity we both racing toward an all-time high. As my wife, Kathy, and I took to the track for the victory lap—the black tar surfacing feeling very much like a frying pan ready for a batch of fried chicken—we joked about how ironic it would be to have survived cancer treatment only to succumb to heat stroke while celebrating. (Such was the gallows humor we had grown accustomed to during cancer recovery.)

What struck me was the word "Hope" emblazed across the front the shirt. I was reminded that hope, from old English *hopa*, means "confidence in the future." Here was a reminder of the challenge of trying to find that confidence during my journey through cancer. There was the hope that the initial x-ray showed a harmless shadow, and not a tumor. There was the hope that I could avoid surgery, that chemotherapy would not be recommended, that side-effects would be manageable, that follow-up tests would be negative, and on and on.

One of the greatest challenges we face as cancer survivors is the balancing act between hope and the "reality" of the illness. For some, the diagnosis itself is enough to extinguish the flame of "everything will be OK." For others, the diagnosis becomes the fuel that turns the kindling of hope into a raging fire of faith. Many, like me, feel the waves of hope rise and fall as a result of the gravitational pull of circumstances. Waiting for test results, I'm surrounded by swells of hopefulness. While wondering if a pain, rash or lump is a sign of the return of the beast brings in a tsunami of "Not again!"

As someone who has entered the cancer journey with a long history of anxiety behind him, I've learned to see hope in a new way. Rather than it being the key to my survival, or, on the other side, a false sense of security, I see it as a reflexive response to uncertainty. As a mechanism for self-preservation, hope arises along with the flight or fight response and works to recalibrate the mind toward its basic instinct for survival. This movement toward equilibrium helps to reset the emotional vibrations in the body that seek harmony in the face of illness.

Thankfully, I've found that hope is there even during times when I've abandoned it. I see it in the eyes of fellow survivors when I return to the oncology office and hear it in the nervous jokes I tell others about the cancer experience. I've come to accept that, even when I'm not feeling very confident about the future, I can still hear that little bird singing, and the tune is music to my ears and my soul.

In Defense of Denial

The art of being wise is the art of knowing what to overlook. -William James

Seven years in to cancer recovery, I'm not able to say that I really remember what life was like before cancer. In my mind I have dreamy images of a life filled with sunny days and hardly a care. Back then, body aches were just the signs of overexertion, doctor's appointments were for stubborn colds and the inevitable breakdowns that come with getting older. Most of all, the "C word" was just that, a word not uttered that always happened to someone else.

My rational mind knows that even before cancer my life was filled with problems, worries, challenges, victories and defeats. Days of sunshine often gave way to dark and stormy moods. All in all, life before cancer was not that different from life after the diagnosis, with one great exception: now I have the realization that the bubble of existence could pop at any moment.

This awareness of the fragility of life, which I've come to see as transformative (the pearl in the muck of this disease), does not always provide a peaceful, easy feeling. While it has driven me deeper into my personal studies into the nature of who and what I am, it can also be a royal pain in the butt. During these times, when I've had it with the existential dilemmas, the metaphysical wrestling match between mind and spirit, I practice the technique that I call *living as if*.

As you've probably guessed, this mode of operating has at its core going about my life as if cancer never happened. This is not revisionist history, it's a deliberate effort to live out the story of my life, in this moment, minus the narrative of the cancer experience. There are four basic rules I try to follow when *living as if*:

1. Denial is my friend and using it consciously means it's not really denial.

2. No looking back at pictures of myself during my hairless chemo days or reading past writings about cancer treatment.

3. Complaining about the small stuff in life is permitted as it feels good to have as the biggest problem of the day be that the cat threw up on the carpet again.

4. Whatever ailment takes center stage is quickly labeled as simply symptomatic of getting old.

I've tried to sell this formula for *living as if* to some of my psychotherapy clients with mixed results. A few see the intended irony that we are already living a life *as if*, and the only change I'm asking them to make is to replace a troublesome story with one that is either positive or, at worst, neutral. Most, however, will push back with some form of wanting to "keep it real." This mantra of a culture

[86]

weaned on the minutia of every happening, reinforces the belief that knowledge is liberating, no matter how painful. I will often respond with the line from Stephen Colbert, who mused, "The more you know, the sadder you get."

Personally, I find these retreats from the "reality" of living after cancer necessary to promote wellness. We survivors are often told not to let our cancer define us, but let's be honest, it's a Herculean task to keep the most traumatic, challenging, heart-wrenching experience from putting a frame around our existence. In many cases it's the frame itself that actually gives our lives meaning. That being said, it's the wise artist who, on occasion, paints a new picture in that frame. There is a great release that comes from allowing the freedom of expression to venture into the surreal; to distort reality to the point where the nightmare of cancer gives way to the dream of pure being.

Man Up! Taking Control of Stubbornness

*There is something in sickness that breaks down
the pride of manhood. -Charles Dickens*

By now, most are aware that when it comes to relationships, "Men are from Mars and women are from Venus." When it comes to how we handle illness, the differences — while not galactic in nature — are notable.

A recent study from the Washington State University pointed out that when it comes to illnesses that have more than one symptom, men cope worse than women. The alarming reality is that according to the American Cancer Society, one in two men are likely to get cancer in their lifetime. Additionally, the mortality rate from cancer is higher for men than for women. Since we know that being a man is, itself, a health hazard, it's time for some serious soul searching. If that sounds too touchy feely, then let's tackle this head-on, man up or maybe we should step up to the plate.

If the traditional male role model is one who is in control, confident and able to go it alone, then we have to face that fact that cancer is an unmanly disease. The trauma of this diagnosis hits most of us men with the one-two punch of an insult to our physical prowess and our mental stability. We're no longer invincible warriors who can stare down the darkest of enemies. Struck by runaway grief, we often flounder in the waters of denial and anger far longer than is healthy. The "never let them know you're hurt" locker room mentality that once served us so well on playing fields only contributes to an increased sense of loneliness and desperation on the uneven surface of a life-threatening illness.

While there are myriad theories that explain men's resistance to asking for help and ignoring personal wellness, they are best summed up by the following road sign:

It's not easy, as a male cancer survivor, to admit that I suffer from stubbornness. In addition to running the risk of getting kicked out of 'the club' for speaking of this, it feels treasonous to call out one's brothers' shared shortcomings. But if pulling back the curtain to reveal that the all-powerful wizard is just a man enables just one of my brothers in cancer to seek help, it will be worth it.

I find this stubbornness in myself, even now. Currently, I'm in the holding pattern of, "Do I really want to know?" as I'm scheduled for an echocardiogram to determine the extent of possible damage to my heart from radiation and a chest X-ray to look for the return of cancer. It's a strange inner battle as the "manly" thing to do would be to say "Bring it on!" However, the other side of my male brain won't allow me to stop to ask for directions has created a list of reasons why I can't keep this appointment.

I know that if something is happening in my body the earlier it's caught, the better. And yet...

Through my years of clinical practice and reviewing my own history as one who carries the burden of the Y chromosome, I've come to the realization that we're a strange bunch. Most boys/men can be talked into the most irrational, dangerous and (let's be honest) insane behaviors by other boys/men with the simple ask, "What, are you chicken?" Proving one's worthiness to wear a "man badge" is so important when in the company of other boys/men that I believe we need to harness this power when it comes to health issues.

 Rather than flooding men with the facts of the dangers of certain behaviors, handing them a list of all of the medical procedures they should have and scaring them with the reality of their mortality rates, we can do the following:

Me: I hear what you're saying doc, but it's a not a good time for me to have this procedure, there's a lot going on at the office right now.

Man doctor: What's the matter? You too scared of a little X-ray? (Starts to cluck like a chicken)

Of course I realize that this approach has multiple flaws, not the least of which is that it first requires showing up at the doctor's office.

In order to help men catch up to women in the health department, we need to take a page from the playbook of our sisters in survivorship. They have known for a long time that reaching out to others, accepting support and sharing their experiences can be lifesaving. If we can get our brothers in arms to reach a hand out to the growing number of men touched by cancer, we may be able to live longer and redefine manhood itself.

Fire Walker: The Initiation of a Cancer Survivor

In the depths of winter, I finally learned that within me there lay an invincible summer. - Albert Camus

"You're going to walk through the fire, and you're going to be OK."

I will never forget these words. They were spoken by a co-worker who had learned that my CT scan had confirmed that there was a mass nestled under my sternum that was not supposed to be there. She pointed to a scar on her right cheek and said, "I got this for my 39th birthday — cancer of the mouth." She hugged me with the kind of the hug that says, "You're one of us now."

I was humbled by her openness and compassion but I was also confused in my denial. What fire? There was no fire, simply some blob that would turn out to be a mere smudge from the radiologist's finger. Or, perhaps, there would just be the low burning ember of, "Well, Mr. Verano, it's not supposed to be there but it's not going to hurt to leave it alone."

Not only were my co-worker's words prophetic, they also pointed to a profound truth. This truth is that life after a cancer diagnosis is never the same, and the challenges ahead are initiation rites of the highest order. Only one who had crossed that blazing bed of charcoal briquettes can possibly look someone in the eye and, without a hint of insincerity, say, "I'll see you on the other side."

There are many ways that illnesses are interpreted. From the "will of God," to random acts of unkindness. Not only are we given a health crisis, we're faced with giving it meaning. What to make of such a mind-numbing diagnosis? Where to turn when life itself it turned upside down?

It's often said that, while our joys make life sweeter, it's our sufferings that define who we are. Despite appearing hardwired for good times, it seems true that it is our pain, not our pleasure, which pushes us toward the "invincible summer." That being said, the road less traveled that is the cancer journey leaves many of us thinking, *I learned a lot about myself going through cancer, but I would have much rather had another teacher.*

Personally, I'm not wired to be a fire walker and crossing the hot coals of this illness drawn on resources that I'm certain are not in my DNA. Long before the attempts to put a philosophical cage around my anxiety, there were the day-to-day challenges of treatment. Even now, I'm at a loss to explain where all the strength, courage and endurance came from, however, I know I borrowed heavily from loved ones and others who have felt similar flames.

Early in my treatment, I often found myself repeating my co-worker's words like a mantra. Especially the "you're going to be OK" part. It had an immediate calming effect, the source of which was much deeper than mere positive thinking. It was as if I was in contact with the spirit in her that had already sorted out the questions, fears and disjointed thoughts that were rattling around in my head. This is the profound gift offered by survivors. Each one shines his or her own light and illuminates the path ahead and separate struggles become one.

Foolproof: On Complementary Practices

Mind-body medicine should not be an 'alternative,' nor should complementary and integrative medicine be something doctors are not exposed to during their training. - Dr. Bernie Siegel

The American Cancer Society refers to complementary and alternative medicine (also known as CAM) as "... terms used to describe many kinds of products, practices, and systems that are not part of mainstream medicine." Later they state that "... you may not hear about these treatments from your doctor or cancer treatment team."

It's clear that cancer is an equal opportunity destroyer, ravaging body and mind. The idea that the CAM model of holistic treatment, with some practices dating back thousands of years, often remains in the muddy waters of "unconventional" seems misguided. Minus the blessing of the medical profession, many of us find ourselves adrift in these waters when it comes to adding methods to treat the whole, not just the parts. When not being brushed aside by the obligatory "We can't recommend that as a treatment," those of us interested in thinking outside of the cancer box are often looked upon as foolhardy.

If you've been through the cancer journey, you've most likely bumped into someone professing the benefits from whatever tools were a part of their recovery. The information and promises can be overwhelming, contradicting and confusing. How does one sift through the plethora of cancer-fighting approaches to find the ones that will actually provide relief and not simply drain one's pocketbook? When does the search for alternatives turn into a fool's errand, and how do we prevent ourselves from getting tricked by treatments?

Full disclosure—I started the cancer journey with a "more is better" mentality. Once the boxes were checked for the traditional methods of surgery, chemo, radiation therapy and medication, I pulled out my mind/body menu and had at it like a starving man at a sushi bar. Here is the complete list of my holistic helpers:

Hatha yoga
Laughing yoga
Meditation/mindfulness
Vitamins
Herbal supplements like Essiac
Qi Gong
Yoga Nidra

Aromatherapy

Smudge stick ceremonies

Bibliotherapy

Bio-Energy healing

Reiki

Telepsychotherapy

Blogging

Prayer/Mantras

Therapeutic massage

I realize it was traditional medicine and the skills of the professionals involved that removed the tumor growing in my chest and destroyed any of its remnants. The addition of complementary practices was used, in most part, to meet the challenges of my side effects and restore a sense of wellness. Whereas chemo drained me of energy and threw my system into a tailspin, yoga, for example, helped to return a sense of balance. I still remember the feeling of accomplishment when, only a week after open heart surgery, I was able to stand in tree pose. If there was even the slimmest chance that any, or all, of the above practices would also decrease the chances of cancer's return; that would be icing on the cake.

Another bonus of jumping on the nontraditional bandwagon is the liberation that comes from no longer being a passive recipient of treatment. Doing things for the mind, body and spirit feels much better than having things done to these vital systems. Additionally, many of these practices can be shared, eliminating the sense of solitary confinement many cancer patients feel sentenced to.

With so many opportunities for misinformation, false promises and profiting from someone else's suffering, my wife and I developed litmus for whatever crossed our radar. Here is the checklist we came up with to eliminate the wheat from the chaff:

1. If it cost more than a 60 minute massage session, it was a "no go" as we found that in most cases, 60 minutes of massage was hard to beat for relaxation and stress reduction.
2. If it came with a promise to cure cancer, we filed it away with the same methods that promised to end aging, regrow hair or create limitless wealth.

3. If the person peddling it looked like the poster child for "don't let this happen to your body," we passed on claims to restore health.

4. If the only evidence for success were anecdotes from the same people who have been taken up in UFOs, we would politely refuse and then add them to the "block sender" list.

[100]

5. If the source was a book that had the words "secret," "hidden" or "forbidden" in its title, it was given a pass in favor of a *Far Side* comic book.

Perhaps the best news about complementary methods is that one does not have to understand, or even believe in, the mechanisms at work to benefit from them. For many, that puts these practices squarely in the category of pseudo-science or snake oil. If pushed on the issue, I will admit I've no scientific proof that anything on the above list aided in my passage from cancer patient to cancer survivor. And while I know that some would argue that they played no role at all, and that to think otherwise is simply fooling myself, my response is, "It feels awesome to be a cancer surviving fool!"

Cancer Fatigue

Our fatigue is often caused not by work, but by worry,
frustration and resentment - Dale Carnegie

I still remember the week after my first round of chemo and radiation, wondering why so many cancer patients described the treatment experience as feeling like the life was being slowly drained out of them. I still had tons of nervous energy, all of my hair and the ability to taste my food. In between appointments, I was busy reporting to work and pulling my fair share. What was all the fuss about? Surely this vampire effect was a myth born from scary stories told by survivors with warped senses of humor.

Then, after the second round, it hit while I was cutting the grass. It was as if someone had pulled the plug and the clear thought in my mind was, "This lawn is going to kill me."

It makes perfect sense to me now that exhaustion is one of the byproducts of cancer treatment. As blood counts drop, cells die, and the mental stress and strain builds, the vital energy force no longer flows like a raging river—it has all the power of a dripping faucet.

Having just enough energy to sit in front of my computer, I was able to Google the experience and was not surprised to learn that it had a name. According to the Mayo Clinic, Cancer Related Fatigue, CRF, "... usually described as feeling tired, weak or exhausted, affects most people during cancer treatment. Cancer fatigue can result from the side effects of treatment or the cancer itself."

There are myriad resources available to help those patients experiencing CRF and I found many of them helpful. What's not as talked about is the exhaustion that comes from living *after* cancer treatment. Factors that impact what I call "survivor related fatigue," SRF, include:

1. Being tired of living with the anxiety of follow-up appointments.

2. Being tired of the chronic aches and pains that result from surgery, chemo and radiation therapies.

3. Being tired of having to keep worries about cancer's return in their mental cage.

4. Being tired of the news of others who have "lost their battle with cancer."

5. Being tired of being tired.

Additionally, as survivors we're often pushed to enter a race against cancer. Whether it's a sprint to a cure, or a competition to live life to the fullest before hitting the finish line, it's a wearisome task that can leave one wondering, "Is this what survivorship is all about?"

Paradoxically, one of the prescribed methods for dealing with CRF is to stay active. Despite the desire to crawl under the covers until the cancer storm blew over, I found that even short walks with one of our dogs did, in fact, counter the walking-dead sensation.

I've found that SRF, on the other hand, is best handled with a compassionate slowing down and learning the art of allowing over forcing, of sensing overthinking. This is not an effort to control the mind or taking on denial as a primary coping skill. This is the practiced effort of being a witness to events—the interested aware presence behind whatever is taking place. The image is that of sitting on the banks of the raging river and resisting the urge to jump in.

While CRF is a product of our physiology, SRF is has its roots in our psychology. Attention is the currency of the mind. When we focus on suffering and loss, we overdraw our reserves, risking mental and emotional bankruptcy. Shifting our awareness and becoming wise investors, not in the future but the present moment, provides a rest stop along the cancer recovery route. Turning our attention toward healing and recovery turns the trivial to meaningful, the minutia to the grandeur, renewing and restoring depleted resources. That this can all be done while sitting silently is good news for the cancer-weary among us.

Here is a brief restorative practice that I was able to use even while lying on the radiation table:

With eyes closed, bring the attention to the flow of breath in and out of the nose or mouth. If a physical sensation arises, let your attention stay there until it is no longer predominant, then return to breath. If thoughts arise, let attention rest there and then return to breath. Take a slow deep breath in to the count of four. Hold the breath for the count of four, and then release the breath to the count of four. Repeat for a series of four cycles and then rest the attention on whatever you are noticing at the moment.

On Life and Living: Cancer and Grief

The most beautiful people we have known are those who have known defeat, known suffering, known struggle, known loss, and have found their way out of those depths.
- Elisabeth Kubler-Ross

In 1969, Elisabeth Kubler-Ross gave us the groundbreaking book, "On Death and Dying." In it, she outlines the five stages of grief — denial, anger, depression and acceptance — as normal reactions to any loss. When one explores the depths of her teachings, it becomes clear that the title of her book could easily have been, "On Life and Living." Far from prescribing a resistance to suffering, up to and including death, she proclaimed, "It is not the end of the physical body that should worry us. Rather, our concern must be to live while we're alive — to release our inner selves from the spiritual death that comes with living behind a façade designed to conform to external definitions of who and what we are."

Those of us touched by cancer know all too well that the stages of grief are not linear and not steps we move along with the precise choreography of ballet dancers. No, these stages represent the roller coaster that has, as an added unnerving thrill, the ability to move in reverse. Thus, today's bargaining gives way to tomorrow's anger, only to be met by yesterday's depression with acceptance waiting patiently on the horizon.

As a therapist, I've found that telling my clients that grieving is essential to their recovery helps eliminate concerns that there is something wrong with being in denial, depressed or angry regarding their illnesses. I try to assist them in finding ways to honor each stage, rather than eliminate it. Knowing that a cancer diagnosis can bring a sledgehammer to the façade that is our self-image, I consider myself both a demolition and hazardous material expert as I join them in the release of inner-self.

When it comes to the stages of grief, my advice to clients has always been that, while there is little we can do to speed up process, there are numerous things that we do to slow it down. These include:

- Lingering too long in any stage on our way to acceptance, and having it become our primary mode of operating.

- Taking on unhealthy coping skills that only reinforce denial, anger and depression.

- Thinking that we have to rush through the stages as if it were a race.

- Trying to reach the peak of acceptance without having traveled through the foothills of resistance.

- Confusing acceptance with "being OK with" or "happy about."

Kubler-Ross wrote, "Those who learned to know death, rather than to fear and fight it, become our teachers about life."

It would be great if we were able to choose both the timing and nature of the lessons that life is trying to teach us. Many of us, however, receive a nudge, push or shove toward the knowledge of our inner selves and thus the meaning of life and death. This suggests there is a natural force working beyond the limitations of our personal understanding. If this is the case and the course in life and living is mandatory (not an elective) then not only am I sitting in the front of the class, I'm taking notes.

Rage Against the Disease

*But grief, and the helplessness it typically brings with it,
are usually not well addressed by allowing the anger to
take the center of the stage.* – Martha C. Nussbaum

I've found in myself, and many of the survivors I've met in counseling sessions, that of all the stages of grief, anger seems to have the greatest staying power. Of course we're angry, and unlike its solemn cousin depression, anger can get us going, fire up the engine and motivate us toward profound acts of courage. Additionally, it has the potential to do the most harm if it becomes entrenched.

The wisdom of Kubler-Ross's work on grief is that, in addition to providing a framework for an experience that is the fate of everyone, it offers a roadmap for those yet to make the trek. In regards to the anger stage, she writes, "It is important to feel the anger without judging it, without attempting to find meaning in it. It may take many forms: anger at the health care system, at life, at your loved one for leaving. Life is unfair. Death is unfair. Anger is a natural reaction to the unfairness of loss."

[111]

This does not mean that we develop a sense of righteous anger where we feel free to share our angst with whoever crosses our path. Nor does it mean that we get to hide behind the false shield of "life hit me first, I was just hitting back." What it does mean is that we drop the need to justify or validate our anger.

Unlike other emotions, we love to question anger. When joyful, how many of us sit around trying to figure out why we're happy? How many of us have read up on how to manage our bliss? Anger is arguably the most analyzed emotion. Ironically, one sure method for complicating a natural and reflexive process is to overthink it. In the sports world, getting distracted by the mind is called "choking." There is a wonderful Taoist expression of this:

When an archer is shooting for nothing, he has all his skill.
If he shoots for a brass buckle, he is already nervous.
If he shoots for a prize of gold, he goes blind or sees two
targets — He is out of his mind!
His skill has not changed. But the prize divides him.
He cares. He thinks more of winning than of shooting–
And the need to win drains him of power.

The last thing any cancer survivor needs is to be drained of any more power than this disease and its treatment steals from us. The key to grieving through the anger stage is to consider the words themselves. Anger comes from Old

Norse *angr*, meaning grief or sorrow. Stage, from the Latin *statum*, means "to stand." Together we arrive at simply standing with our sorrow; no rants or rages, no destructive acts of violence, just a natural reaction to the unfairness of this disease.

Psychologists learned the hard way, that the conventional wisdom of acting out anger, i.e. hitting a pillow, or punching bag, etc. actually creates the effect where anger simply boomerangs back to lodge itself in our psyches. A simple way of expressing this would be; anger out, anger in. Those of us survivors who carry the extra burden of the Y chromosome know that men naturally gravitate toward the "If it angers you, break it" mentality. I personally felt this impulse during the days when the steroids introduced to manage side effects of chemo were playing havoc with my attempts to get all Zen with my treatment.

What's an angry, cancer-hating, chemically enhanced survivor to do when we find ourselves as the primary star under the spotlight on the anger stage? First and foremost, it's important to remember that not judging does not mean swallowing anger where it can fester only to reappear as yet one more physical ailment. Secondly, it means that we do not judge ourselves for experiencing moments where we feel we could chew iron and spit nails. Other useful tips for exiting the anger stage include:

1. See anger as a call to attend to a problem, not as the problem itself.
2. Use anger energy as motivational strength to take action.
3. Dilute the negative effects of anger by laughing more.
4. Address the feelings of helplessness that lies at the root of anger through acts of compassion toward self and others.
5. Stop blaming yourself for getting angry; blame is just anger in another disguise.

As a final note, I've noticed that occasionally some cancer survivors will turn their anger toward other survivors who attempt to find the positive in the cancer experience. On the receiving end, it can feel like unduly harsh criticism for simply not giving in to the impulse to rage against the disease. From the sender's perspective, the, "cancer is my friend," crowd are steeped in denial and quite possibly insane. As someone who, most of the time, resides on the receiving end, I would never try to rob someone of their right to feel anger. Rather than return fire, I understand that it's not me they are angry with, it's our common foe, cancer, and rather than their enemy, I feel like an ally.

The Commercialization of Cancer

Years of love have been forgot, in the hatred of a minute.
-Edgar Allen Poe

There is a new cancer center commercial that, quite frankly, freaks me out. At first, I thought it was just me being upset that my zone-out time watching golf (I know, it's hard to get more couch potato than that) was interrupted several times by cancer. I realized that it was not just the "pardon the interruption" component when my wife overheard the commercial and had the immediate response, "Turn that off. That's so wrong. You can't talk to cancer like it's a person!"

I feel the need to preface this rant with acknowledging that, of course, I feel for the people in this commercial. They are, reportedly, real survivors and real physicians and I send my blessings and peace to all of them. The script they were given, however, leaves me feeling like someone has jumped on the political bandwagon and created the first attack ad against cancer.

If you've not seen it, I'll sum it up for you. During the ad several cancer survivors take turns telling cancer off. The tone varies between defiance and disgust and, for me, had the quality of fingernails on a blackboard.

In a time when mudslinging and vitriol are running wild, do we really need to get all "in your face" about cancer and its treatment? Is hating cancer and what it has taken from us really going to move us forward in understanding the mechanisms involved in cancer cell growth? Will warning cancer that "we're after it" lead us to less devastating forms of treatment? Personally, I prefer that those involved in the process come at with a more compassionate, questioning and determined attitude than that of "Cancer, you suck!"

Whether we will defeat cancer in this, or any, lifetime is certainly a question worth asking. And if anyone should have a say in the matter, survivors and family members who've lost loved ones to the disease should top the list. When those voices are put together in a collage and then entered into the public discourse, I think we owe it to everyone to keep that dialogue sane, civil and useful.

Since I was not consulted prior to the commercial being released, I would like to, with tongue firmly in cheek, offer two pitches for the next advertisement:

Pitch #1:

Scene opens to reveal a chemotherapy room. Chairs are arranged in a circle, with IV poles and monitors next to each. Chairs are empty, and dim sunlight filters the room with a warm glow. In complete silence, a nurse walks across the room, pauses for a moment at each chair, and then walks over to the only monitor still on. The camera zooms in on the face of the monitor and the nurse flips the "off" switch. She walks out of the room, closes the door, and is seen hanging a sign just below the words Treatment Room. We hear her footsteps fade out as the camera zooms in on the sign that reads, "Going Out of Business."

Voice over: (I'm thinking James Earl Jones-like) "Working toward the day."

Pitch #2:

Viewers see me (I always wanted to be on TV) sitting on the couch, with my Great Dane, Daphne, curled up next to me. Looking straight into the camera with a serious look on my face, despite the dog gnawing on a red snake chew toy, I say, "Hey cancer, I wanted to have a word with you, and then I realized you're not a person, and talking to you might not make any sense. Not only do you not have ears, mouth, eyes or nose, you also have no soul." I turn and start talking to dog. "Isn't that right, girl? Cancer ain't got no soul." I grab the chew toy, look it straight in the eyes and say, "Ain't that right snake?" I squeak the toy and hand it back to the dog.

Scroll comes up reading, *Brought to you by the Council for Compassionate Cancer Care (4C). We foresee* (I really should get paid to do this) *a life free of cancer.*

Half-Empty: A Pessimist's Guide to Cancer

Both optimists and pessimists contribute to our society. The optimist invents the airplane, and the pessimist the parachute. – George Bernard Shaw

Of all the balancing acts performed by cancer survivors, walking the thin and shaky line between optimism and pessimism may be the most precarious.

During the early stages of cancer treatment, I felt attempts to keep my glass half full, though the power of positive thinking was being equally matched by the half-empty reality of this disease. Hopes of a benign tumor were replaced by the shock of malignancy, while affirmations for a less invasive procedure were countered by orders for the full-frontal assault of thoracic surgery. On and on it went, increasing the fear that my optimism balloon was about to pop.

Ironically, what kept my positive hopes afloat was not resisting the pull toward the dark side, but allowing my inner cynic to see occasional daylight.

As a psychotherapist who believes in the power of positive psychology, I'm acutely aware that our thoughts shape our lives. I am familiar with the research that points out that

[119]

optimists often heal faster, have better immune systems and are happier in the long run. I'm also aware of neurological studies that suggest that our brains are wired for a negativity bias that keeps new, and potentially harmful, experiences from being our last. We would not have lasted very long as a species if our optimistic ancestors had used positive thinking in the face of a charging saber-tooth tiger, rather than thinking the worst and allowing the natural reflex of fight or flight to kick in.

Finding the silver lining in the dark cloud of cancer can feel like a fool's errand, despite the seemingly instinctive need to keep hope alive. Added to our own reflexive straining to see the bright side, are the wishes, needs and demands of loved ones that we stay upbeat. Though well-intended, this can lead some to conclude that pessimism is a sign of weakness, of giving up the cancer fight. Internalized, this can lead to feeling that the fault of their cancer lies not in the stars, but in themselves.

Coming face-to-face with a cancer diagnosis not only shakes the very ground beneath one's feet, it sends tremors throughout the mental landscape that constitute one's worldview. If that view is one where the grass is always greener, nice guys always finish first and good things happen to good people, it can be hard to see the big picture through the tears. Since sadness is a poor motivator, a heaping dose of pessimism can be a good antidote for the poisonous reality of the moment.

The positive side of a negative outlook is that it can spur one to take action, provide the impetus for needed change and help one marshal the resources for meeting a challenge. Additionally, exposing one's inner pessimist to the light of day can be a healing ritual in the same way that turning a light on removes the frightening dark shadows from a room. The day I was finally able to give voice to my deepest fear about my upcoming chemo and radiation therapies, I felt that in that moment, I had exorcised a demon that had effectively withstood the onslaught of positivism.

As someone who entered the cancer arena prewired for anxiety, I'm a firm believer in the use of the psychological maneuver known as defensive pessimism. This constructive use of negativity has been shown to reduce anxiety by developing plans for dealing with the worst-case scenario rather than trying to will oneself into a positive frame of mind. Let's face it, telling an anxious mind to not worry and just be happy is as useful as trying not to get wet in a rainstorm by thinking sunny thoughts. It's better to just open the umbrella.

Whether or not we enter cancer survivorship with our glasses half-full or half-empty, it's helpful to remember that we need not choose a side in order to maintain wellness. I've discovered that the best answer to the question, "Are you an optimist or a pessimist?" is "Yes."

Grace Under Pressure: Facing the Follow-Up Visit

Courage is grace under pressure. - Ernest Hemingway

As a cancer survivor, I find that I don't always measure up to papa Hemingway's ideal. Despite often lacking both courage and grace, I somehow still manage to do the brave thing. This is particularly true every time I face a follow-up appointment to check for cancer's return.

Every time I enter the, *Star Trek*-like, capsule that is the CT machine, I go in less like the brave Captain Kirk, and more like Major Weenie. "Boldly go where no man has gone before"? I think not.

Unpredictability is par for the course when it comes to a cancer diagnosis. However, I have found a strange comfort in a very reliable pattern when it comes to preparing for follow-up visits:

One year out: I receive the news that my last scan was negative, schedule the follow-up scan and rest easy thinking, "It is 365 days away; that's a long time."

Six months out: The date for the scan has Freudian-slipped my mind, and it still feels a long way off.

Three months out: I start thinking, "I should probably find my appointment card that has the date on it and put it on my calendar." I convert months to days as ninety feels better than three of anything.

One month out: The appointment is officially on my work calendar and I'm careful not to schedule anything too mentally draining that day. Previous experience tells me that I will not be fully-functioning that day.

Two weeks out: Every bump and every body ache is surely my cancer returning, I can feel it growing even as I sleep. What's that large lump? Wait, it's the dog.

Three days out: I can barely feel my toes as the blood is pooling in my brain, trying to figure out ways to cancel the appointment.

If history repeats, I will gracefully keep my next appointment. While there, I will think of all of those other survivors who have returned to their battlegrounds and felt the strange sense of déjà vu all over again. I will probably make an awkward attempt at humor as the technician sticks me with a needle to see what my blood's been up to. I will put on my best brave face and walk out as if waiting for the results is just another thing on my "To Do" list. No one will be buying it; but that's what I'll be selling.

[124]

Between now and then, I will rest easier knowing that my wife, Kathy, will be sending positive energy vibes my way (these have proven to be even more powerful than radiation) and that family and friends are keeping me in their thoughts and prayers. I will consider what Hemmingway said about courage and come to the realization that I prefer what John "Duke" Wayne said, "Courage is being scared to death but saddling up anyway." Now that, I get. Giddy up!

Moving On

In three words I can sum up everything I've
learned about life: it goes on. – Robert Frost

The question, "How do you move on?" was simple enough and seven years into cancer survivorship I should have knocked it out of the park. It came from a cancer survivor, one year out of cancer surgery. I've thought, talked and written about this very topic for years, so I was stunned to hear myself sputtering out phrases like, "You just do," and "Life is what moves you on." Fortunately, the question came at the end of a counseling session so I punted with the phrase "that's a good place to pick up the next time we meet."

Conventional wisdom and training suggests that therapists should be wary of answering direct questions. It one of the things that, ironically, drives people crazy in therapy — their questions are always answered by another question. As a cancer-surviving therapist, it seemed like too much of a psychological two-step to answer a question about living with the fear of cancer's return with something as banal as "tell me what you think."

The trap I had unintentionally laid for myself, however, was thinking that there was some magic combination of words that could unlock this mystery or act as a healing balm. I know very well that my own sense of "moving on" had nothing to do with being given some positive affirmation or, even worse, a catchphrase. I understand deep in my core that there were countless variables involved in moving from surviving into thriving.

Later that evening, as I reflected on my attempt to put into words something ineffable, I became fixated on the very phrase "move on." There are many ways that survivors are encouraged, prodded and cajoled toward the idea that in order to fully recover from cancer we need leave the role of cancer patient behind. In psychological circles this is often referred to as "closure," but in the real world it's better known as "get over it" or "let it go."

Thirty-plus years into the practice of psychotherapy, I've learned that telling someone that their recovery depends on "moving on" is akin to telling a depressed person to just "be happy." My approach these days is to talk about living with rather than living without, allowing over forcing and, most importantly, realizing that life moves on in wellness and illness, joy and suffering, pleasure and pain. I firmly believe that illness does not halt this process; it does not put the brakes on existence. Feeling stuck comes from a trick of the mind that sees suffering, of any kind, as an unnecessary detour and waste of time.

Once we allow our lives to unfold with cancer as part of our experience, we awaken to the literal meaning of the word survive which is "to live beyond." This is the wisdom of being told that we become survivors on the day we receive our diagnosis. Thus, the need to discover the way ahead, to put psychological, emotional and spiritual distance between ourselves and the illness is already being met. Therefore, the work is often a matter of staying out of our own way as we move through this process.

That I momentarily lost my understanding that we can to live our down times with as much vigor, interest and compassion as our up times is no longer a surprise. Upon reflection, I understand that I was trying to help my client, not support her. I wanted to clear the road rather than walk it with her. I saw the hurdle of anxiety and wanted to knock it down — all of this despite my Zen understanding that the obstacle is the path.

I made a commitment to myself that I will not be caught off guard again. I've developed my, ever at the ready, response for the next time I'm asked some version of "How do you move on?" The answer is in three parts, and in true psychotherapist fashion in the form of questions.

1. Where do you want to go?

2. How will you know it when you get there?

3. How can I help you along the way?

Coping with the Trauma of Cancer

And the day came when the risk to remain tight in a bud
was more painful than the risk it took to blossom.
- Anaïs Nin

"It feels almost like PTSD." This was not the first time I've heard a cancer survivor describe the experience this way, but it struck a deeper chord this time. I've been thinking a lot lately about the traumatic impact of living with a cancer diagnosis and the stresses and strains of its treatment on one's mental health.

One of the reasons I've been mulling over the relationship between cancer and PTSD is that I've recently been certified in the trauma response known as critical incident stress management, or CISM for short. Briefly put, those of us trained under the auspices of the International Critical Incident Stress Foundation (ICISF) serve as first responders providing psychological first aid to those exposed to a traumatic event. The other reason is my personal experience going through cancer treatment as a licensed therapist made me disappointed by the lack of awareness about its impact on my emotional wellbeing.

Through contact with other survivors and some quick online research, I learned that I was not alone in wondering about the lack of interest in the stress I was experiencing. According to the book, *Cancer Care for the Whole Patient: Meeting Psychosocial Health Needs*, "...the remarkable advances in biomedical care for cancer have not been matched by achievements in providing high-quality care for the psychological and social effects of cancer.

Numerous cancer survivors and their caregivers report that cancer care providers did not understand their psychosocial needs, failed to recognize and adequately address depression and other symptoms of stress, were unaware of or did not refer them to available resources, and generally did not consider psychosocial support to be an integral part of quality cancer care."

According to the ICISF, critical incidents that can lead to acute stress or a post-traumatic stress disorder are defined as, "unusually challenging events that have the potential to create significant distress and can overwhelm one's usual coping mechanisms." Can a survivor get an "amen!?"

While normally thought of in terms of natural disasters like hurricanes and floods, or the man-made variety like mass shootings and terrorist attacks, it is by no means a psychological stretch to see how a cancer diagnosis fits the bill of a critical incident. It's not uncommon to hear a survivor refer to receiving the diagnosis as his or her personal 9/11 or tsunami.

If it's true that cancer can pull the rug out from underneath the most sane and rational among us, why is it not also true that we respond with the psychological equivalent of CPR, or, at the very least, an emotional Heimlich maneuver?

If, as the American Cancer Society projects, there will be more than 20 million cancer survivors by 2026, there are going to be a lot of folks living in a state of acute or post-traumatic stress. We need only consider the vast number of veterans who are leaving wars zones in the Middle East with the ravages of PTSD to appreciate the importance of staying ahead of this curve to honor those who will join battle against cancer.

Perhaps, what we need, in addition to the Vice President's "Moonshot" to cure cancer, is an equally down-to-earth response to address the mental health of those still waiting for the cure. I can't be the only one to see the irony in attempts to save the body from being taken over by rogue cells only to have one's emotional and mental life cause such suffering so as to give rise to the lament of, "Is this what I survived cancer for?"

The great news is that we have proof that early intervention with trauma not only helps to restore previous levels of functioning and improve chances for recovery, but it also aids in what is known as post traumatic growth (PTG). Coined by Richard Tedeschi and Lawrence Calhoun in 1995, PTG is, "positive change experienced as a result of the struggle with a major life crisis or a traumatic event." PTG moves us out illness and into wellness as it becomes the blessing within the curse.

Imagine a time when, upon receiving a cancer diagnosis, a person is given access to a trained professional whose primary role is to provide the necessary mechanisms for improving resistance, resilience and recovery. Put in simpler terms—how great would it be to have someone teach cancer patients the skills that are essential to no longer feeling like a cancer patient?

Until the day when we have, at the ready, trained professionals to provide psychological assistance to anyone who receives a cancer diagnosis, here are some tips for developing an at-home psychological first aid kit.

1. Keep something comforting close by. From pets to cherished photographs, worry beads to religious images, surround yourself with whatever helps provides a sense certainty and stability.

2. Have emotional Band-Aids handy. Personally, I found that music, soothing scents and Ben & Jerry's ice cream were the mental equivalent of an Ace Bandage.

3. Consider a pain reliever. Antidepressants and anti-anxiety medications can address the mental pain caused by stress, anxiety and/or depression that can inhibit healing and recovery. While I hear from many survivors that the last thing they want is to take another medication, why would we avoid treating the psychological side effects of cancer with medicine any more than the nausea?

4. Heal old wounds. If there are lingering issues from your past that negatively impact how you experience your present moment, consider seeking professional help. There is no need to add to the cancer burden by still lugging around old baggage.

5. Educate yourself. Take a break from learning more about your cancer and seek out information on how others cope with adversity. Become a scholar in resiliency or head directly into the field of trauma recovery.

6. Research on the use of psychological first aid has shown that it is often best administered by peers. Combine this with the understanding that helping others has a profound impact on one's own wellbeing,

and the silver lining in the dark cloud of cancer is that the war against it is creating an army of first responders who know first-hand how to help heal cancer-induced trauma.

Seriously? Finding the Lighter Side of Cancer

Laughter and tears are both responses to frustration and exhaustion. I myself prefer to laugh, since there is less cleaning up to do afterward. - Kurt Vonnegut

Looking back over some of my recent writing, I was astounded by the lack of humor. The serious tone and, dare I say, preachy quality made me pause and reflect. When did I stop being funny? I don't feel that one has to take on a solemn tone when approaching cancer. As a matter of fact, I have always believed that a sense of humor was a key element when trying to dodge the slings and arrows along the path of most resistance. What gives?

Upon further reflection, I realized I had fallen prey to one of the lesser known side effects of going through the cancer journey. This side effect, unlike the ones that come along with chemotherapy, arises solely from the mind and has a full-proof remedy. The symptom is to feel the heaviness of life, and the cure is to simply lighten up.

Let's be honest, on the surface there is nothing funny about cancer. Having to face this demon head-on is no laughing matter and someone needs to take it very seriously if we are ever to see the day when we can use the word "cure." Still, who says that one cannot strive for a higher cause while taking the low road of slapstick comedy? Where is it written that we can't take the "mean" out of meaningful and just have a good laugh now and then?

It was Oscar Wilde who said, "Life is far too important a thing ever to talk seriously about." He wasn't kidding. Or maybe he was? Who knows? Who cares? It's a great quote.

We are repeatedly told that laughter is the best medicine. Of course there are times when the joke not only is lost on us, it seems that we are the very butt of the joke. It's the feeling that the punch line has hit us right in the solar plexus, or, in my case, right in the thymus gland, which is just a little higher. It's ironic that this profound sense of humor would leave us just when we need it most.

The problem lies with confusing serious with important and funny with trivial. When strength of conviction hardens, it loses its flexibility and can no longer smile. In rigid fashion it pooh-poohs the free-spirited, spontaneous, take-life-as-it-comes approach. (Pooh, now that's a funny word).

I've seldom heard a cancer survivor or survivor of other traumas, for that matter, exclaim: "You know, I find that I'm a lot funnier now after what I've been through."

Maybe that means it's time to take on a viewpoint best expressed by the recently departed, Robin Williams: "I'm not laughing at you, I'm laughing near you." Tragedies can bring a heavy-heartedness to our lives so why not counter with a lighter heart? If we're going to head into the deep waters of the meaning of life after a cancer diagnosis, why not strap on the laughing gas along with the oxygen tank?

It is most likely some innate wisdom — and not-so-subtle reminder — that tears accompany both a good cry and good laugh. Surely, in both cases they spring from the same profound source of — you thought I was going to get all deep there, didn't you? Seriously?

The Healing Power of "Why?

It is not the answer that enlightens, but the question.
- Eugene Ionesco

My guess is that it's crossed your mind countless times but maybe never crossed your lips. If not, allow me to do it for you: Why?

There, I said it. I hope it brings you even a moment's relief as it does for me when I get over the strange idea — the origin of which escapes me — that as cancer survivors, we're not supposed to ask why it happened to us, or to anyone, for that matter. So strong is the backlash against this question that it may as well join the ranks of other unmentionables and simply be referred to as the "W" word.

One often hears cancer survivors proclaim with pride, honor and dignity, "I never asked why this happened to me." Unintentionally, this sets the standard for those who follow, creating the unwritten rule that asking why is to admit weakness, to be unfit for battle. It's as if one is about to go AWOL in the war against cancer. As anyone knows, good soldiers do not question their duty, they simply do it. Any good recruit knows that the proper response to "Jump!" is not "What for?" but "How high?"

As a psychotherapist, I'm privileged to meet with people in some of their most unguarded moments. During these sessions, their need to understand their suffering is palpable. Sitting like balloons on pins and needles, it's not hard to get them to pop. When I give a struggling client permission to verbalize the profound question mark they brought into the room, I can feel the shift in energy. I see the relief in their eyes and the burden lightened on their shoulders.

Due to the power of cultural conditioning, many of the people I meet not only need permission, they need me to lead them in the refrain. It's almost as if they're seeking assurance that they will not be struck by a lightning bolt for having the audacity to say out loud that which is lodged in their brains. If I have an adventurous soul in my midst, will we chant the mantra: "Why me, why now, why this?"

The reason there is a healing power in "why?" is that it shines a light into the dark recesses of the questioning mind itself. Neuroscience tells us that our minds are wired to scan the happenings around and within, and look for signs of change. It's an evolutionary skill that helps increase the chance of seeing another sunrise. Trying to tame this curiosity by pushing it below the level of conscious awareness is the psychological equivalent of trying to hold a beach ball under the water, only minus the sun and fun. Allowing fears to surface is to exhale the inner tension and catch our breath as we prepare for the next wave to wash over us.

In my own survivorship, I've found that when it comes to the big ticket questions in life, the advice from the poet Rainer Maria Rilke keeps things in perspective. In addressing a struggling young poet, he advises:

"Do not now look for the answers. They cannot now be given to you because you could not live them. It is a question of experiencing everything. At present you need to live the question. Perhaps you will gradually, without even noticing it, find yourself experiencing the answer, some distant day."

Coming to terms with being a survivor of cancer means, in large part, the willingness to live the question of why this happened to me. It is making peace with that "distant day" and finding the courage to stumble toward it, if we have to. When we understand that seeking is fundamental to healing, we turn the very question back on itself: Why ask why? Why not?

[143]

The Dos and Don'ts of Waiting on Test Results

Time is not a thing that passes ... it's a sea on which you float. - Margaret Atwood

Whoever said there's no way to make time stand still clearly never had to endure the excruciating wait for scan results. In an age of instant everything, cancer patients being told that the data from the cutting edge technology that is creating real-time images of our innards will be available in anything less than a nanosecond defies logic and seems unnecessarily cruel.

I underwent a PET scan last Thursday. And I'm here to assure all naysayers out there that not only did time stand still, but it even moved backward.

Immediately upon leaving the mobile scan machine, it was once again 2009 and I was walking out of my first CT scan trying to read the faces of the technicians who had monitored the process. What did they see? Could I tell from the demeanor whether or not the results were good or bad? What were they not telling me? It was déjà vu all over again, including the numbness in my toes— a sure sign that my brain was calling on all blood cells.

[145]

During these frozen moments in time, it's hard to think about plans for a future that may not be. We're told that at this present moment, it is the focus at the heart of the meditation/mindfulness movement that promises to end mental anguish. As a believer and meditation teacher, however, I am here to tell you that if that moment is wrapped in a cocoon of worry about whether or not you have to go through chemo and radiation therapies again, then the "oh no!" factor is like walking across hot coals with gasoline shoes.

When the word finally came that the scan showed no changes, aka, "you get to live a little longer," I was literally stunned by relief. It was as if the movie of my life had been kicked out of freeze frame and I was back in the flow. Sitting back down to lunch with my wife, who, as a result of my taking the call outside so as to not cause a scene in the restaurant, should one be necessary, was in a state of panic, we ate as if it were our last, and first, meal.

There was a strange silence between us as if the celebration of life had been rained on by the unnecessary struggle with uncertainty over the last four days. We did manage a toast to health, and once again cursed the evil bastards who, in my cynical mind, think nothing of taunting those of us challenged by cancer with our very survivorship.

Settling back into what is now my "new normal," I decided I would create a "Do and Don't" list for the next time I'm faced with the deafening silence of waiting on test results:

Don't – Sit still. This is not a time for seated meditation on the nature of your breath.

Do – Move. Get off your butt and put your body in motion. Remember, it's harder for bad news to hit a moving target.

Don't – Stop planning for the future, including what you're going to have for dinner.

Do – Realize that all of our planning, cancer or no cancer, is based on the *assumption* that we're going to be around in the future.

Don't – Waste any time trying to feel where in the body your cancer has mostly likely returned.

Do – Remember that if you could self-diagnose, you'd have magic powers that you could sell over the Internet.

Don't – Make promises to whatever higher power you believe is in charge of the universe that you will make wholesale changes to your life in return for a good test

[147]

result. Reneging on a promise to the big "I am" is bad karma.

Do – Make a promise to yourself to use your time (however much that is) to bring joy, lightness and ease into your life and the lives of all those you touch.

Playing the Cancer Card

The best way to pay for a lovely moment is to enjoy it.
– Richard Bach

Let's face it, there are very few good things that come with a cancer diagnosis. In fact, the effort to turn the sour lemon of this diagnosis into anything that even remotely resembles lemonade requires a Herculean effort and/or a touch of the miraculous.

One of the methods my wife and I developed toward of the cynicism that comes when faced with such an unrelenting foe is something we call "playing the cancer card." Playing the cancer card, PCC to us insiders, is simply introducing the fact that one is going through, or has gone through, the cancer experience at a time when it seems to be in one's interest to do so. This should not be confused with taking advantage of the kindness of others. Instead, what we're doing is allowing others to express their genuine concern and caring and, in return, gaining the heartfelt sense of having done a good deed. It's truly a win-win— a rare occurrence in the cancer world.

During active treatment, the cancer card actually plays itself. I paid for zero meals while going through chemo and radiation therapies. I assume that friends were just so happy to see that I still had an appetite, despite not being able to taste most of what I was eating and, during the worst of the esophagitis, making everything swallowed feel like broken glass, that they were totally eager to donate to the cause. While going through the tell-tale no hair look, it was clear that even passing strangers were kinder, giving up places in line, extending cordial greetings instead of blank stares and even the occasional "stay strong" encouragement.

Once one is out of the treatment woods and the obvious markers of "cancer patient" give way to a healthier survivor glow, PCC is a good tool for keeping the dark thoughts at bay. Used with a sense of playfulness, the subtle, or not so subtle, reminder that one is a member of the cancer club becomes a way to honor what one has been through without turning into the bitter survivor that no one wants to be around.

Personally, I have pulled the cancer card in the following scenarios:
- While public speaking and getting the sense that the audience is growing weary of the topic I'm covering. Very few people will give bad reviews to a speaker who has shared his cancer experience.

- When forgetting an important date involving a close friend or family member. "My bad, I think I was just coming out of chemo fog during that time."

- When trying to get "street cred" with someone who has been through some really tough life challenges. I was told by a rough-and-tumble client who I had shared my survivorship with, "Where I'm from, you get mad respect for that."

Like all card games, there are rules for PCC that one should follow so as to not scare away the truly caring people we need as part of our recovery:

1. Never PCC when angry. I tried this once after getting a really bad meal during my active treatment and it took me months to stop feeling like a jerk.

2. Always keep in mind that you may be dealing the cancer card to someone whose life is far more of a train wreck than yours.

3. Let others in on the joke that your use of PCC is really a defense mechanism to ward off the heebie-jeebies that come with cancer.

4. Remember that the Joker is a wildcard in PCC and that not everyone sees the humor in making fun of such a deadly disease.

5. If you're going to PCC with another cancer survivor, decide ahead of time that it will be a draw and that in the end, we're all winners.

Reframing the Cancer Experience

Life is a series of natural and spontaneous changes.
Don't resist them - that only creates sorrow. -Lao Tzu

The crushing blow of a cancer diagnosis can bring about dramatic changes in one's view of both the external and internal worlds. In an attempt to bring order to the chaotic shifts taking place, the mind will often take necessary liberties with the truth. In psychotherapeutic terms, these reality makeovers are called reframes. They are a very powerful tools that not only help turn lemons into lemonade, but also help to reorient one toward a path of recovery and wellness.

The mother of all reframes in the cancer world is the "Cancer is the best thing that ever happened to me" mantra. This clearly takes the bitter pill of a potential life-ending ailment and places it gingerly in the sweeter, more digestible, category of life-altering. The reasons that reframing works so well are: a) there is a degree of truth in the statements and b) rather than being a fixed element, reality is what each one of us decides it will be.

[153]

An old Zen story points to the notion of reality being in the mind of the beholder. Here is a reworked version from the vantage point of a cancer diagnosis:

A worried patient seeks the counsel of a wise Zen master and complains, "An awful thing has happened. I've been diagnosed with cancer. What have I done to deserve such a fate?" The Zen master replies, "It's hard to say what it good or what is bad." The next week, the patient returns and exclaims, "A wonderful thing has happened! Since being diagnosed with cancer I no longer worry about simple things. Isn't that great!" Once again the Zen master replies, "It's hard to say what is good and what is bad." The next week, a despondent patient sits at the feet of the master and laments, "Such horrible news – I've been so focused on my treatment I forgot to pay my mortgage, I risk losing my home. When will these tragedies end?" The Zen master smiles and replies, "It hard to say what is good and what is bad."

Obviously, the story could go on indefinitely with each new triumph and tragedy being met with the same response. The existential unpinning of the vignette is that the world is made up of opposites that, in truth, do not oppose, but support each other. It is not a matter of this *or* that, but this *and* that. Therefore, if we choose, cancer is both the worst and best thing to happen to us.

[154]

Since the rotation of the world's opposites leave many feeling dizzy, seeking refuge at the still focal point is a reasonable antidote to motion sickness. The time-honored trick of "fix your gaze on the horizon" is appropriate as one looks beyond chemo and radiation therapies, blood tests and dying cells to the distant day when life is no longer being tossed by the tidal waves of emotions.

A great teacher once exclaimed, "The mind is a cheat, seek refuge in the heart." My psychotherapeutic pronouncement of this truth is, "Your mind has no second thoughts about playing tricks on you; feel free to play back." There is no rule that says we have to take on the thorns of the world if we are feeling depleted, distressed and depressed. I actively encourage all my clients experiencing life-altering stressors to trick the mind using the art of reframing.

The energy that is freed up by choosing a less stressful "truth" can be directed toward seeking refuge in the heart. It is there that we realize that cancer is only one of countless experiences that shape our existence. Within this inner-knowing, the question, "Is it good or bad?" is moot. We don't even need to be, or visit, a Zen master to open this sanctuary – our cancer has provided the access.

Back to the Moon: On Becoming a *Cancernaut*

And the goal of this initiative — this "Moonshot" — is to seize this moment. To accelerate our efforts to progress towards a cure, and to unleash new discoveries and breakthroughs for other deadly diseases. - Joe Biden

I was 8 years old when we first stepped on the moon. Even at that young age, I knew that it meant we were living in a new world. I watched as the marvels of the space age, and I don't just mean the wonder that was Tang™, sprung up all around us.

As a seven-year survivor of a rare thymic cancer, I feel like that 8-year-old child again as I think about the possible future as we start the new cancer moonshot, proposed by Joe Biden. When I unexpectedly joined the cancer program just before my 50th birthday, I was sure I had the "right stuff" to meet the challenge. However, I was reluctant to join the arms race that is the war on cancer. I'm a pacifist to my core, and the battle against cancer never seemed like a fair fight.

Thanks to the moonshot initiative, I can now adopt a frame of reference for survivorship that feels like a perfect fit. I prefer to think of myself as an explorer,

[157]

a "cancernaut," if you will, boldly going where many have gone before, only this time with the nation and the world cheering me on.

President Kennedy told the nation that the original moonshot would ". . . serve to organize and measure the best of our energies and skills, because that challenge is one that we are willing to accept, one we are unwilling to postpone, and one which we intend to win."

One has to wonder what would have happened if President Kennedy chose the battle theme for our quest. My guess is that if he had replaced "I believe that this nation should commit itself to achieving the goal, before this decade is out, of landing a man on the moon and returning him safely to the Earth" with declaring a "war on gravity," we'd still be wondering if the moon is made of cheese.

How can we expect anything less than new wonders once we unleash the powers of our new technological age on this deadly disease? How can we not feel the swell of pride in the realization that we stand at a turning point in human history?

Let's face it, the final frontier is not the depths of space, but the depths of the human experience. For too long, cancer has left its mark on this experience, often having the last word. The attempt to silence this voice through an all-out war has left many of us feeling like refugees, rather than heroes. With this new endeavor, we can rise above our reflexive tendency to fight fire with fire, and, instead, light the flame of inspiration and hope for millions.

It makes perfect sense, in a war weary world, to adopt a new paradigm for treating cancer. Imagine the possibilities when we turn rage into enthusiasm—when the summary of a cancer survivor's life no longer opens with the line, "He lost his battle with cancer," but instead, "He took living with cancer to new heights."

It should be no surprise that it took someone whose life was deeply impacted by the cancer experience to finally create a paradigm shift in how we approach a cure for this illness. The idea of marshaling our country's resources and engaging the best and brightest in an all-out effort to cure cancer stands in stark contrast to the war mentality.

If we look at the historical record of our success rates with our previous wars on poverty, drugs and terrorism, it seems that dislodging our efforts to cure cancer from that frame of mind would decrease the chance of failure. Wars are notorious for pouring valuable resources into bottomless wells where the original cause often gets lost amongst conflicting priorities. The moonshot analogy, on the other hand, speaks to a unified purpose and the coordination of resources toward a clearly defined target. Anyone who has ever watched a NASA-related movie knows, "Failure is not an option." Now that's the kind of boosting power we survivors have been dreaming of.

Of course, much like the original space race, the vice president's plan has its naysayers. *The New York Post* put it this way: Biden's cancer 'moon shot' is a grand idea that's doomed. Others have jumped on the let's-abort-the-launch bandwagon with explanations that run the gamut of the political spectrum.

I, for one, will not let these wet blankets dampen my enthusiasm for what could be a turning point. I prefer being associated with a pioneer in a space program than a soldier in a war. I love the idea that one giant leap for mankind in the search for a cure for cancer may mean many more small steps will be taken by millions of survivors around the globe.

To those who are already trying to point out the dark side of this new moonshot by suggesting that cancer is too complex and too difficult a disease to set such an unrealistic goal, I would remind them of President Kennedy's words at the start of space race:

"We choose to go to the moon. We choose to go to the moon in this decade and do the other things, not because they are easy, but because they are hard, because that

[160]

goal will serve to organize and measure the best of our energies and skills, because that challenge is one that we are willing to accept, one we are unwilling to postpone, and one which we intend to win, and the others, too."

Now that's a battle cry to get behind. Let's not wait another moment to shoot for the moon. In the words of the first American into space, Alan Shepard, let's "light this candle."

The Emperor Has Old Clothes

No emperor has the power to dictate to the heart.
- Friedrich Schiller

The Pulitzer Prize winning author, Siddhartha Mukherjee, refers to cancer as the "emperor of all maladies." This seems a fitting title for an illness capable invading the healthiest of bodies and conquering all in its path with such malevolence that most dare not even whisper its name. In Harry Potter-like fashion, the, "name that shall not be named," has been reduced to simply "the C word."

While cancer is often thought of as a disease of modern life, as Mukherjee points out, it is "...one of the oldest diseases ever seen in a human specimen -- quite possibly *the* oldest." Since this tyrant has been with us throughout the ages, one might expect that the treatment of it would mirror the miracles of medicine that have led to the pronouncement of the other, often unspoken, word; cure.

The historical record of cancer remedies and treatments reads like a horrific tale of terror and torture. From bloodletting, to the non-anaesthetized surgical removal of tumors, early attempts to eradicate the growing menace speak to both the depth of fear it instilled and the dedication of those determined to eradicate the threat once and for all.

We have taken giant leaps forward in the understanding of cancer and moved out of the darkened shadows of exploratory and often deadly interventions into the light of scientifically sound targeted therapies. Despite this, any cancer survivor knows that the confirmation of a cancer within one's body is only the beginning of the dark night of the soul. Personally, I have often repeated the line, "I was never really afraid that I would not survive cancer, but I was convinced that chemotherapy would kill me."

While it would take thousands of years before war was officially declared on cancer, the battle lines were drawn early in human history and the ravages of this war only add to cancer's dark legacy. If one was lucky enough to survive the crude assaults on the body; archaic attempts to literally carve out cancer free zones, the same fortune may falter in the face of infections in a pre-antibiotic age.

When it comes to cancer and its treatment, what's old is new. Despite astounding medical advances, the disease continues to carry the weight of a death sentence and its treatment comes at the cost of living cells and tissues. Anyone who has sat through the first round of chemotherapy, and the obligatory recital of the list of possible side-effects, most likely leaves with the thought

[164]

that was pounding in my head when I returned for my second session, "I can't do this anymore."

It's far too easy to throw up our collective hands and raise the white flag of surrender to cancer. With more than just a hint ironic respect for cancer's shape-shifting nature, Mukerjee, at the end of his fascinating work, points out that cancer may be ". . . the new normal--and inevitability." The question, then, he adds is "not *if* we encounter this immortal illness in our lives but *when*." For millions of cancer survivors like myself that *when* is *now*.

If history teaches us anything, it is that all empires, and those that rule over them, eventually collapse under the weight of their own vanity. Let us both praise and bury Caesar by exhausting all efforts to strip cancer of its power to rob, pillage and plunder what is most precious—the undying spirit of life that is truly immortal.

Let's do this by living with dignity despite cancer's attempts humiliate us. Let's continue to create unity when cancers tries to isolate us. Let's live from our hearts while cancer confounds the mind. Finally, let's refuse the "new normal" where illness reigns and instead live the realization that love is the ultimate conqueror and the heart our true home.

About the Author

Mike Verano was diagnosed with a rare form of thymic cancer in 2009. He is a licensed therapist, certified employee assistance professional and recovering *stressoholic* with over thirty years of experience in the mental health field. A self-proclaimed pacifist in the war on cancer, Mike is dedicated to helping those going through the cancer experience find safe-havens for creating wellness. He and his wife Kathy live in Virginia.